I0008546

Hands-On Spring Security 5 for Reactive Applications

Learn effective ways to secure your applications with Spring and Spring WebFlux

Tomcy John

BIRMINGHAM - MUMBAI

Hands-On Spring Security 5 for Reactive Applications

Commissioning Editor: Richa Tripathi
Acquisition Editor: Chaitanya Nair
Content Development Editor: Zeeyan Pinheiro
Technical Editor: Ruvika Rao
Copy Editor: Safis Editing
Project Coordinator: Vaidehi Sawant
Proofreader: Safis Editing
Indexer: Aishwarya Gangawane
Graphics: Jason Monteiro
Production Coordinator: Shantanu Zagade

First published: July 2018

Production reference: 1310718

Published by Packt Publishing Ltd.
Livery Place
35 Livery Street
Birmingham
B3 2PB, UK.

ISBN 978-1-78899-597-9

www.packtpub.com

First and foremost, I would like to thank my savior and lord, Jesus Christ, for giving me strength and courage to pursue this project.

I would like to dedicate this book to my father (Appachan), the late C.O. John, and my dearest mom (Ammachi), Leela John, for helping me reach where I am today. A special thanks to my dearest wife, Serene, and our three lovely children, Neil (son), Anaya (daughter) and Hazel (our newborn sweet baby girl - DOB 18.07.18), for all their support throughout this project and also for tolerating not being with them after my busy day job. Last but not the least, I would like to thank my uncle (Appappan), Thomaskutty C.O, who took the initiative to introduce me to a variety of books during my studies.

`mapt.io`

Mapt is an online digital library that gives you full access to over 5,000 books and videos, as well as industry leading tools to help you plan your personal development and advance your career. For more information, please visit our website.

Why subscribe?

- Spend less time learning and more time coding with practical eBooks and Videos from over 4,000 industry professionals

- Improve your learning with Skill Plans built especially for you

- Get a free eBook or video every month

- Mapt is fully searchable

- Copy and paste, print, and bookmark content

PacktPub.com

Did you know that Packt offers eBook versions of every book published, with PDF and ePub files available? You can upgrade to the eBook version at `www.PacktPub.com` and as a print book customer, you are entitled to a discount on the eBook copy. Get in touch with us at `service@packtpub.com` for more details.

At `www.PacktPub.com`, you can also read a collection of free technical articles, sign up for a range of free newsletters, and receive exclusive discounts and offers on Packt books and eBooks.

Contributors

About the author

Tomcy John is an enterprise Java specialist with over 16 years of several domain expertise. He is currently a part of the Emirates IT Group as a Principal Architect. Before this, he's worked with Oracle Corporation and Ernst & Young. He acts as a chief mentor to facilitate incorporating new technologies. Outside of work, he works closely with young developers and engineers as a mentor and speaks on topics ranging from web and middleware all the way to various persistence stores. Tomcy has also the co-authored a book on big data, *Data Lake for Enterprises*, which is published by Packt.

It was my privilege working with my technical reviewer, Ranga Rao Karanam. I would like to thank my mentors (Karthic Sundararaj, VP IT Architecture Emirates Group IT; and Rajesh R.V, Chief Architect Emirates Group IT), teachers, friends, and my extended family for their support in me to reach this stage in my career, with words of encouragement and wealth of knowledge at all times. I would like to thank my entire Packt team (Chaitanya, Zeeyan, and Ruvika) for their support and this opportunity. Lastly, I would like to thank everyone who stood besides me during this entire journey.

About the reviewer

Ranga Rao Karanam is a programmer, trainer, and an architect. He is the founder of in28Minutes, helping 2 million learners re-skill on cloud-native applications, microservices, evolutionary design, high quality code, DevOps, BDD, TDD, and refactoring. He loves consulting for start-ups on developing scalable component-based cloud-native applications and following modern development practices such as BDD, Continuous Delivery, and DevOps. He loves the freedom the Spring framework brings to developing enterprise Java applications.

> *First of all, I should congratulate Tomcy on a wonderful book. I loved reading the book and have picked up some new thoughts/concepts. It's one of the best technical books I've read in the last quarter. Coming from a bibliophile like me, it's quite a compliment.*

Packt is searching for authors like you

If you're interested in becoming an author for Packt, please visit `authors.packtpub.com` and apply today. We have worked with thousands of developers and tech professionals, just like you, to help them share their insight with the global tech community. You can make a general application, apply for a specific hot topic that we are recruiting an author for, or submit your own idea.

Table of Contents

Preface

Security is one of the most difficult and high-pressured concerns of creating an application. The complexity of properly securing an application is compounded when you must integrate this with existing code, new technologies, and other frameworks. This book will show readers how to easily secure their Java applications with the tied-and-tested Spring Security framework, the highly customizable and powerful authentication and authorization framework.

Spring Security is a well-known and established Java/JEE framework that can provide enterprise-grade security features for your application with no trouble. It also has modules that enable us to integrate with a variety of authentication mechanisms, and we will be delving into each of those using hands-on coding in this book.

Many examples will still be explained using the Spring MVC web application framework, but will still have a flavor of reactive programming to them.

Reactive programming is gaining traction, and this aspect of Spring Security will be covered by showcasing Spring Security integration with the Spring WebFlux web application framework. In addition to reactive programming, the book will also delve into other Spring Security features in detail.

Finally, we will also bring in some of the products available on the market that can be used along with Spring Security to achieve some of the security features needed in modern applications. These products offer new/enhanced security capabilities, and work in harmony with Spring Security in all aspects. Some of the products discussed are also fully endorsed and supported by the Spring community.

Who this book is for

This book is for anyone who fits into the following groups:

- Any Spring Framework enthusiast who would like to integrate Spring Security into their application
- Any passionate Java developer who would like to start using one of the very core modules of Spring Framework; namely, Spring Security

- Experienced Spring Framework developers who would like to get their hands dirty with the newest Spring Security module and would also like to start coding applications with the reactive paradigm

What this book covers

Chapter 1, *Overview of Spring 5 and Spring Security 5*, introduces you to the new application requirements and then introduces you to reactive programming concepts. It touches on application security and what Spring Security brings to the table to address security concerns in an application. The chapter then gets into a bit more into Spring Security and then finally closes by explaining how the examples in this book are structured.

Chapter 2, *Deep Diving into Spring Security*, deep dives into the technical capability of core Spring Security; namely, Authentication and Authorization. The chapter then gets your hands dirty with some example code, in which we will set up a project using Spring Security. Then, in due course introduces you to the approach by which the code samples will be explained throughout the book.

Chapter 3, *Authentication Using SAML, LDAP, and OAuth/OIDC*, introduces you to three authentication mechanisms; namely, SAML, LDAP, and OAuth/OIDC. This is the first of two main chapters, in which we will dive deep into various authentication mechanisms supported by Spring Security using hands-on coding. We will be explaining each authentication mechanism using a simple example to cover the crux of the topic, and we'll be keeping the example simple for easy understanding.

Chapter 4, *Authentication Using CAS and JAAS*, introduces you to two more authentication mechanisms that are very much prevalent in enterprises—CAS and JAAS. This is the second of the two main chapters, similar to Chapter 3, *Authentication Using SAML, LDAP, and OAuth/OIDC*, which will initially cover the theoretical aspects of these authentication mechanisms. This chapter concludes the topic by implementing a fully-fledged example using Spring Security.

Chapter 5, *Integrating with Spring WebFlux*, introduces you to one of the new modules introduced as part of Spring 5—Spring WebFlux. Spring WebFlux is a web application framework in the Spring ecosystem that was built from the ground up to be fully reactive. We will bring the reactive parts of Spring Security out in this chapter and will also detail the Spring WebFlux framework itself. First we will introduce you to Spring WebFlux using an example and then we will build on the additional technical capabilities on top of the base application.

Chapter 6, *REST API Security*, starts off by introducing you to some of the important concepts in regards to REST and JWT. It then introduces OAuth concepts and, using hands-on coding examples, explains simple and advanced REST API security, focusing on utilizing Spring Security and Spring Boot modules in Spring Framework. The examples will use the OAuth protocol and will be using Spring Security to the fullest to secure REST APIs. In addition to that, JWT will be used to exchange claims between the server and client.

Chapter 7, *Spring Security Add-Ons*, introduces many products (open source and paid versions) that can be considered for use alongside Spring Security. These products are strong contenders that can be used to achieve the technical capability that you are looking for in your application to cover various security requirements. We will introduce a product to you by giving you the gist of the technical capability that needs addressing in your application, before taking a look at the product in question and explaining how it provides the solutions you require..

To get the most out of this book

1. The book contains a number of examples, all coded and executed in a Macintosh machine using an IDE (IntelliJ). So, to follow the examples easily, usage of macOS and IntelliJ would help a great deal. However, all code can be executed using Macintosh, Windows, and Linux systems.
2. Basic to intermediate experience working on applications built using Java and Spring Framework is required to progress through the book easily.

Download the example code files

You can download the example code files for this book from your account at www.packtpub.com. If you purchased this book elsewhere, you can visit www.packtpub.com/support and register to have the files emailed directly to you.

You can download the code files by following these steps:

1. Log in or register at www.packtpub.com.
2. Select the **SUPPORT** tab.
3. Click on **Code Downloads & Errata**.
4. Enter the name of the book in the **Search** box and follow the onscreen instructions.

Once the file is downloaded, please make sure that you unzip or extract the folder using the latest version of:

- WinRAR/7-Zip for Windows
- Zipeg/iZip/UnRarX for Mac
- 7-Zip/PeaZip for Linux

The code bundle for the book is also hosted on GitHub at `https://github.com/PacktPublishing/Hands-On-Spring-Security-5-for-Reactive-Applications`. In case there's an update to the code, it will be updated on the existing GitHub repository.

We also have other code bundles from our rich catalog of books and videos available at `https://github.com/PacktPublishing/`. Check them out!

Download the color images

We also provide a PDF file that has color images of the screenshots/diagrams used in this book. You can download it here: `https://www.packtpub.com/sites/default/files/downloads/HandsOnSpringSecurity5forReactiveApplications_ColorImages.pdf`.

Conventions used

There are a number of text conventions used throughout this book.

`CodeInText`: Indicates code words in text, database table names, folder names, filenames, file extensions, pathnames, dummy URLs, user input, and Twitter handles. Here is an example: "`Flux<T>` is a `Publisher<T>` with basic flow operations and supports *0..n* elements."

A block of code is set as follows:

```
public abstract class Flux<T>
    extends Object
    implements Publisher<T>
```

Any command-line input or output is written as follows:

```
curl http://localhost:8080/api/movie -v -u admin:password
```

Bold: Indicates a new term, an important word, or words that you see onscreen. For example, words in menus or dialog boxes appear in the text like this. Here is an example: "Enter the username as `admin` and password as `password` and click on **Sign in**."

Warnings or important notes appear like this.

Tips and tricks appear like this.

Get in touch

Feedback from our readers is always welcome.

General feedback: Email `feedback@packtpub.com` and mention the book title in the subject of your message. If you have questions about any aspect of this book, please email us at `questions@packtpub.com`.

Errata: Although we have taken every care to ensure the accuracy of our content, mistakes do happen. If you have found a mistake in this book, we would be grateful if you would report this to us. Please visit `www.packtpub.com/submit-errata`, selecting your book, clicking on the Errata Submission Form link, and entering the details.

Piracy: If you come across any illegal copies of our works in any form on the Internet, we would be grateful if you would provide us with the location address or website name. Please contact us at `copyright@packtpub.com` with a link to the material.

If you are interested in becoming an author: If there is a topic that you have expertise in and you are interested in either writing or contributing to a book, please visit `authors.packtpub.com`.

Reviews

Please leave a review. Once you have read and used this book, why not leave a review on the site that you purchased it from? Potential readers can then see and use your unbiased opinion to make purchase decisions, we at Packt can understand what you think about our products, and our authors can see your feedback on their book. Thank you!

For more information about Packt, please visit `packtpub.com`.

Overview of Spring 5 and Spring Security 5

This book expects readers to be conversant with Spring Framework (any version) and Spring Security (any version). This is an ice-breaker chapter that introduces the reader to some of the most important concepts; we will expand on them in subsequent chapters.

The chapter will introduce you to new application requirements and then to reactive programming concepts. It touches on application security and how Spring Security addresses security concerns in an application.

We'll continue with Spring Security and then close the chapter by explaining how the examples in this chapter are structured. This is quite important as I expect readers to be comfortable whenever a new concept is introduced in code.

In this chapter, we will cover the following topics:

- New-generation application requirements
- Reactive programming
- Reactive applications
- Spring Framework
- Reactive landscape in Java
- Spring Framework and reactive applications
- Application security
- Spring Security
- Spring Security's core features
- Spring Security 5's new features
- The working of Spring Security
- Core Spring Security modules

How examples are structured

It's important that you understand how we will be using examples in this book. Since the book tries to give lots of detail on Spring Security 5 and its reactive aspects, we will not have a single use case throughout the book. Instead, we will keep creating small projects to help you understand each of the core concepts covered. Here are some of the important aspects of the code base within this book:

- Most concepts will be covered using a standalone Spring Boot project.
- At times, we will use the famous Spring Initializr (`https://start.spring.io/`) to bootstrap our sample Spring Boot application. In other cases, we will start with a base project that we already have and introduce more concepts through code.
- Generally, we will be using Java configuration. At times, we might use XML-based configurations.
- We will keep our examples as simple as possible so that we don't lose focus on the core concept being introduced.
- Even though this book is focused on reactive applications, we will not be covering this each time it is introduced. At times, we will just be doing plain, old imperative programming as it is more important to know reactive programming and use it when required. It's not that we have to use reactive code everywhere possible, just use it where you see fit.
- We will be using VS Code for all the projects, and we'll be using the extensions available in VS Code to the fullest. We will also be using the Spring Initializr extension rather than using online Spring Initializr.
- We will be using Maven most of the time in this book. There might be a case where we try Gradle.
- Sometimes, we might use IntelliJ IDE and you'll see some screenshots showing this.
- We'll be using the latest Spring Boot release version, namely **2.0.0. RELEASE**. This is the latest release version of Spring Boot at the time of writing this book.

New-generation application requirements

Here are some of the core new application requirements:

- **Highly scalable**: The social platform has grown exponentially over the last decade and people are more tech-savvy than ever.

- **Resilient, fault-tolerant, and highly available**: downtime in your application is something which enterprises are not ready to take in modern times; downtime of even seconds is now creating huge losses for many big businesses.
- **High performance**: If your site is slow, people have a tendency to leave and search for alternatives. People have a short attention span and will not stay or come back if your website performs poorly.
- **Hyper-personalization**: Users need personalized websites rather than generic websites, and this puts huge pressure on servers to do many intensive analyses in real time.

With technology in everyone's hands (in some form or another, most people use technology), users are quite well-versed in privacy policies and application security. They are aware of most of the security requirements, and companies take time to educate users about the importance of security and the ways they should look for security flaws in applications. You might already know that if a site runs on HTTP as opposed to HTTPS (SSL) and Chrome tags, these sites quite clearly show the users as **Not Secure** in the address bar. With more people becoming knowledgeable about technology, these aspects are well-known among the majority of users and security has become one of the most talked about subjects in the IT landscape.

Another important aspect is data privacy. Some users are not concerned about sharing their data but some are quite reticent. Many governments recognize this fear and have started making many rules and regulations in this space. One such data privacy rule is the well-known **General Data Protection Regulation** (**GDPR**), which has been enforced since May 25th, 2018.

The **European Union** (**EU**) GDPR replaces the Data Protection Directive 95/46/EC and was designed to harmonize data privacy laws across Europe, to protect and empower all EU citizen's data privacy and to reshape the way organizations across the region approach data privacy. For more information, you can check this link: `https://gdpr-info.eu/art-99-gdpr/`.

Modern browsers have also given us enough tools to look at many aspects of a web application in a more detailed manner with regards to security. In addition, browsers have been enhanced with more and more features (for example, a cookie was once one of the options for storing data, but now we have other options, such as **localStorage** and **indexedDB**), making it more vulnerable to security breaches and attacks from an ever-open hacker sitting on the sidelines.

To achieve these various application requirements, organizations go to public cloud providers instead of their own on-premise datacenters. This puts applications in a more vulnerable state and security aspects come to the forefront. The various components that constitute the application need to be highly secured and nonhackable.

The technological landscape is constantly growing, with new technologies popping up and getting adopted by the developer community. Because of this and the various technology improvements it brings in, many organizations have to adopt these technologies to be compete within the market. This again puts huge pressure on security, as these shiny new technologies may not have concentrated enough effort on making security a major requirement.

All in, having rigid security in an application is a no-brainer requirement and organizations, and end users, are well aware of this fact.

Reactive programming

Over the last few years, JavaScript has become one of the most used languages, and you have already heard of the term **reactive** in the world of JavaScript, both in a backend and a frontend context.

So, *What exactly is reactive programming?*—It's a programming paradigm that has asynchronous data streams at its core. The data flows through various parts of the program in the form of a message. The message is produced by a `Producer` and works in a fire-and-forget manner in which the program produces a message and forgets it. The `Subscriber` who has subscribed (shown interest) to such messages, gets the message, processes it, and passes on the output as a message for other parts of the program to consume.

In the world of databases, NoSQL presented a huge shift from relational databases. Similarly, this programming paradigm is a huge shift from the conventional programming paradigm (imperative programming). The good thing is that without much knowledge, you have already been coding a bit of reactive code in your day-to-day coding life. Wherever you see the word **stream**; you are indirectly using a piece of reactive code. Such programming has a name of its own and this aspect has become more mainstream in the industry. Many languages understand the advantages this brings and they have started to natively support this paradigm of programming.

Reactive applications

In the earlier section of this chapter, we covered how application requirements have drastically changed over the last decade. To cater to this, there is a concept of application development named reactive applications.

It is important to understand the difference between reactive programming and reactive applications. Employing reactive programming doesn't produce reactive applications, but concepts of reactive programming can definitely aid in building reactive applications.

Knowing the Reactive Manifesto will help you understand reactive applications/systems because the manifesto clearly dictates each and every aspect of reactive applications.

Reactive Manifesto

A **manifesto** is a public declaration of intentions, opinions, objectives, or motives, as one issued by a government, sovereign, or organization (http://www.dictionary.com/browse/manifesto).

The **Reactive Manifesto** clearly articulates the views of the issuer, following which an application can be developed to be reactive.

According to the Reactive Manifesto (https://www.reactivemanifesto.org/), a reactive system should be responsive, resilient, elastic, and message-driven.

Let's get into each of these terms in a bit more detail. Most of the text in this section is from the online Reactive Manifesto and then slightly modified to convey the concepts in more easily digestible terms for the readers.

Responsive

In case of problems, responsive systems can quickly detect them and effectively deal with them. These systems also give consistent response times and also establish upper bounds, guaranteeing a minimum **Quality of Service (QoS)**. Because of such characteristics, these systems build end user confidence, simplify error handling, and encourage more interaction from end users.

Resilient

In the case of failure, resilient systems stay responsive and interactable. **Resilience** in an application can be achieved by:

- **Replication**: Running the same component in more than one place, so that if one fails, another could handle it and the application can function in a normal fashion.
- **Containment/isolation**: Issues of a particular component are contained and isolated within that component and don't interfere with other components or other similar components spun up as part of replication.
- **Delegation**: In the case of an issue in a component, without much deliberation, the control is transferred to another similar component that is running in a completely different context.

Elastic

Elastic systems can easily autoscale (increase or decrease resources) as the input rate increases or decreases. Such systems don't have any contention points and can replicate components at will, distributing the increase in load. The way these systems are designed makes sure that when scaling is required, it can be done in a very cost-effective manner by adding on more commodity hardware and software platforms as opposed to expensive hardware and licensed software platforms.

Message-driven

In reactive applications, one of the main aspects is the usage of asynchronous messages to pass data from one component to another. This brings loose coupling between components and aids in achieving location transparency (as long as the component is reachable/discoverable, it can reside in a single node or a cluster of nodes anywhere). Create a message, publish, and forget. Registered subscribers receive the message, process it, and broadcast the message for the other subscribes to do their jobs. This is one of the core aspects of reactive programming and it is one of the fundamental aspects needed for a reactive system. This fire-and-forget concept brings in a non-blocking way of communication, resulting in highly scalable applications.

The following diagram (*Figure 1*) clearly shows the Reactive Manifesto in a pictorial fashion. It also clearly shows the relationship between the main concepts on the Reactive Manifesto:

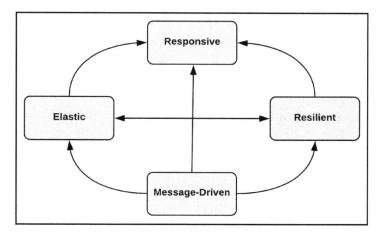

Figure 1: Reactive Manifesto

Since reactive applications are responsive, resilient, elastic, and message-driven, these applications are inherently highly flexible, highly scalable, loosely coupled, and fault-tolerant.

Mateusz Gajewski, in one of his presentations shared on `www.slideshare.net`, sums up the Reactive Manifesto in a very nice way:

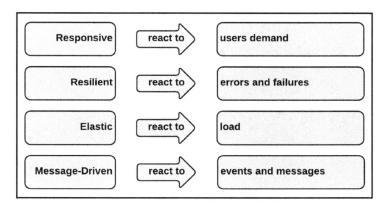

Figure 2: Reactive Manifesto as conceived by Mateusz Gajewski

Spring Framework

Spring Framework is the de facto standard for building Java applications. Over the last decade, it has matured with every major release. Spring Framework 5 became generally available as 5.0.0. in September 2017; this is an important release (major) for the framework since its previous version, which was released in 2013.

One of the major additions to Spring 5 is the introduction of a functional web framework, Spring WebFlux, built on the core reactive foundation. Reactive programming is slowly creeping into the framework and many core modules within the framework are inherently supporting reactive programming in a big way. Since the framework has started supporting reactive programming natively, core aspects of this programming are fully implemented and followed by many of the modules. Also, many reactive concepts have become common language within the framework.

It's important to note that Spring's reactive concepts have been taken as is from Java 8's **Reactor Core library**, which implements the reactive programming paradigm. Reactor Core is built on top of *Reactive Streams Specification*, which is the industry standard for building reactive applications in the Java world.

Another important feature is the inclusion of new way by which such applications can be tested. We have a dedicated chapter for Spring WebFlux in (Chapter 5, *Integrating with Spring WebFlux*) where these aspects will be covered in more detail.

Being a major release, it has loads of stuff either added or enhanced. But we are not going to list all of its features. The full list can be found at this link: https://github.com/spring-projects/spring-framework/wiki/What%27s-New-in-Spring-Framework-5.x.

Reactive Landscape in Java

It's hard to wrap your head around reactive concepts when you're coming from a traditional programming model. Some of the subsequent sections are aimed at introducing you to reactive concepts and how they evolved into their present state.

Reactive Streams and Reactive Streams Specifications

The official document for Reactive Streams (`http://www.reactive-streams.org/`) says that—*Reactive Streams is an initiative to provide a standard for asynchronous stream processing with non-blocking back pressure. This encompasses efforts aimed at runtime environments (JVM and JavaScript) as well as network protocols.*

It started as an initiative between a group of companies in 2013. In April 2015, 1.0 of the specification was released and there were a number of implementations (such as Akka Streams and Vert.x) available at the same time. The specification was initiated with a target to get it included in the official Java standard library and in 2017, with the release of JDK9, it made it's way into it officially. As with any specification, the ultimate aim is to have a number of implementations conforming to the specification, and over time, the specification evolves. The specification consists of some core interfaces, some rules around these, and a **Technology Compatibility Kit (TCK)**.

TCK is a suite of tests that will be executed to check the correctness/compliance of a **Java Specification Request (JSR)** implementation. In **Java Community Process (JCP)**, TCK is one of the three required components for ratifying a JSR. The other two are JSR specification and JSR reference implementation. The TCK for the Java platform is called **Java Compatibility Kit (JCK)**.

Being a specification, it enables any implementation respecting the specification to cooperate and interoperate with each other. For example, an implementation written in Akka can talk to the Vert.x implementation over the Reactive Streams protocol without any trouble. Adoption is growing and, as we speak, more implementations that conform to the specifications written in different languages are being released:

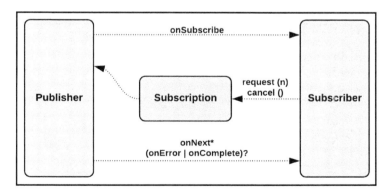

Figure 3: Reactive Streams Specification/API

The preceding figure clearly shows the **Reactive Streams Specification**. Some of the important specification rules are as follows:

- The calls from `Publisher` to `Subscriber` and `Subscriber` to `Publisher` shouldn't be concurrent in nature.
- The `Subscriber` can perform its job synchronously or asynchronously but always has to be non-blocking in nature.
- From `Publisher` to `Subscriber` there should be an upper bound defined. After that defined bound, buffer overflows occur and could result in errors.
- Apart from **NullPointerException** (**NPE**), no other exception can be raised. In the case of NPE, `Publisher` calls the `onError` method and `Subscriber` cancels the `Subscription`.

In the preceding definition of Reactive Streams, there are some very important terms, namely **non-blocking** and **backpressure**, which we'll explore a bit more to understand the core concepts of Reactive Streams.

Non-blocking

Non-blocking means threads never block. If the thread needs to block, the code is written in such a way that the thread gets notified at the right time and the process continues. Reactive programming lets you implement a non-blocking, declarative, and event-driven architecture.

One of the approaches to writing non-blocking applications is by using messages as the means of sending data. A thread sends the request and soon after that, the thread is being used for something else. When the response is ready, it is delivered back using another thread and the requesting party is notified so that further processing can continue:

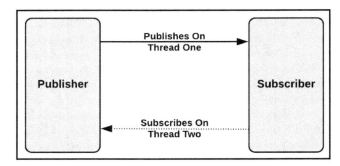

Figure 4: Non-blocking

The non-blocking concept is already implemented by well-known frameworks, such as Node.js and Akka. The approach that Node.js uses is a single thread that sends data in a multiplexing aspect.

In telecommunications and computer networks, multiplexing (sometimes contracted to muxing) is a method by which multiple analog or digital signals are combined into one signal over a shared medium. The aim is to share an expensive resource. For more information about multiplexing, you can visit the following link: http://www.icym.edu.my/v13/about-us/our-news/general/722-multiplexing.html.

Backpressure

In an ideal scenario, every message produced by the `Producer` is passed to the `Subscriber` as and when the message is produced without any delay. There is a chance that the `Subscriber` is unable to handle the messages at the same rate as they are produced and this can cramp its resources.

Backpressure is a method by which the `Subscriber` can tell the `Producer` to send messages at a slower rate to give the `Subscriber` time to handle these messages properly without putting too much pressure on its resources.

Since this is the first chapter, we are just introducing you to these important reactive concepts. Code examples will be covered in subsequent chapters.

Now that we have a brief idea of Reactive Streams and Reactive Streams Specification, we will go into next important reactive concept in Java, namely Reactive Extensions.

Reactive Extensions

Reactive Extensions (Rx or ReactiveX) (https://msdn.microsoft.com) is a library for composing asynchronous and event-based programs using observable sequences and LINQ-style query operators. Data sequences can take many forms, such as a stream of data from a file or web service, web services requests, system notifications, or a series of events such as user inputs.

As stated in the preceding definition, these are APIs that allow stream composition using the Observer pattern. It's my duty to introduce you to the Observer pattern before going any further. The following is the definition of this pattern and it's quite intuitive

The Observer pattern defines a provider (also known as a subject or an observable) and zero, one, or more observers (`Subscriber`). Observers register with the provider, and whenever a predefined condition, event, or state change occurs, the provider automatically notifies all observers by calling one of their methods. For more information about the Observer pattern, you can refer to this link: `https://docs.microsoft.com/en-us/dotnet/standard/events/observer-design-pattern`.

Data can flow in a number of forms, such as streams or events. Reactive Extensions lets you convert this dataflow into observables and aids you in programming reactive code.

Rx is implemented in a variety of languages, including Java (RxJava). A full list of implemented languages and more detail on Rx can be found at `http://reactivex.io/`.

RxJava

RxJava is a Java VM implementation of ReactiveX—a library for composing asynchronous and event-based programs by using observable sequences.

RxJava was ported from .NET to the world of Java by Netflix. After almost two years of development, a stable release of the API was made available in 2014. This stable release targets Java (Version 6 and above), Scala, JRuby, Kotlin, and Clojure.

RxJava is a single-JAR, lightweight library and focuses on Observable abstraction. It facilitates integration with a variety of external libraries, making the library align with reactive principles. Some examples are `rxjava-jdbc` (database calls using JDBC with RxJava Observables) and Camel RX (Camel support for Reactive Extensions using RxJava).

Reactive Streams and RxJava

RxJava 2.x is a complete rewrite from its predecessor, RxJava 1.x.

RxJava 1.x was created before Reactive Streams Specification, and because of this it doesn't implement it. RxJava 2.x, on the other hand, is written on top of Reactive Streams Specification and fully implements it, and also targets Java 8+. RxJava types in RxJava 1.x have been fully tweaked to comply with the specification and suffered heavy changes when the rewrite took place. It's good to note that there exists a bridge library (`https://github.com/ReactiveX/RxJavaReactiveStreams`) that bridges between RxJava 1.x types and Reactive Streams, allowing RxJava 1.x to pass the Reactive Streams TCK-compliance tests.

In RxJava 2.x, many concepts remain intact but names have been changed to comply with the spec.

We will not be going deep into RxJava as it is a big topic and there are plenty of books available that dive deep into RxJava.

JDK 9 additions

As part of concurrency updates to JDK 9 (JEP 266), Reactive Streams was added to the Java standard library. Reactive Streams was initiated in 2013 by some of the well-known organizations that wanted to standardize the approach by which asynchronous data can be exchanged between software components. Soon, the concept became adopted by the industry and there evolved a number of implementations that all had similar core concepts but lacked standard nomenclature and terminologies, especially as regards interfaces and package naming. To avoid multiple nomenclatures and to enable interoperability between implementations, JDK 9 included basic interfaces as part of the **Flow Concurrency** library. This made applications want to implement Reactive Streams to depend on this library but not include specific implementations into the code base. Thus it is very easy to swap between implementations without any trouble.

These interfaces are coded as static interfaces within the `java.util.concurrent.Flow` class.

Important interfaces

Reactive Streams specifications in Java 9 revolve around just four interfaces—`Publisher`, `Subscriber`, `Subscription`, and `Processor`. The library also includes a `Publisher` implementation—`SubmissionPublisher`. All of these are included within the `java.util.concurrent` package in the Java standard library. We will touch upon these interfaces in the following subsections.

The Publisher Interface

The definition of this interface is as follows:

```
public interface Publisher<T> {
  public void subscribe(Subscriber<? super T> s);
}
```

As you can see, `Publisher` allows the `Subscriber` interface to subscribe to it so as to receive the message when `Publisher` produces it.

The Subscriber Interface

The definition of this interface is as follows:

```
public interface Subscriber<T> {
  public void onSubscribe(Subscription s);
  public void onNext(T t);
  public void onError(Throwable t);
  public void onComplete();
}
```

As you can see, the `Subscriber` interface's `onSubscribe` method allows `Subscriber` to be notified when `Publisher` accepts the `Subscription`. The `onNext` method is invoked when new items get published. As the name suggests, the `onError` method is invoked when there's an error and the `onComplete` method gets invoked when `Publisher` has completed its function.

The Subscription interface

The definition of this interface is as follows:

```
public interface Subscription {
  public void request(long n);
  public void cancel();
}
```

The method request is for accepting requests for items and method cancel is for when `Subscription` is cancelled.

The Processor interface

The definition of this interface is as follows:

```
public interface Processor<T, R> extends Subscriber<T>, Publisher<R> {
}
```

It inherits from both the `Publisher` and `Subscriber` interfaces and therefore inherits all the methods of these interfaces. The main aspect is that the `Publisher` can produce an item but the `Subscriber` can consume a different item than that produced by the `Publisher`.

Spring Framework and reactive applications

Spring Framework adopted reactive in 2013 (the same time reactive was born and became more mainstream) with the release of Version 1.0 of Reactor. This was the time when Spring Framework Version 4.0 was released and Spring got itself engaged with **Pivotal**. In 2016, Spring's 4.3 Version was released with Reactor's Version 3.0. Around this period, the work on Spring's Version 5.0 (major version) was actively under construction.

With new-generation application requirements, many conventional coding practices were challenged. One of the main aspects was to get rid of blocking IO and to find an alternative to conventional imperative programming.

Web applications backed by a Servlet container are inherently blocking, and Spring 5 did a great deal in web application development by introducing a fresh web application framework based on reactive programming: Spring WebFlux.

Spring also has embraced Rx and has used it in many ways within Spring 5. With Spring 5, reactive features are baked into it in many aspects, helping developers to embrace reactive programming easily in a slow-paced manner.

Pivotal is heavily invested in Reactor but has exposed APIs, allowing developers to choose the library of their choice between Reactor and RxJava.

The following diagram depicts Spring 5's reactive programming support:

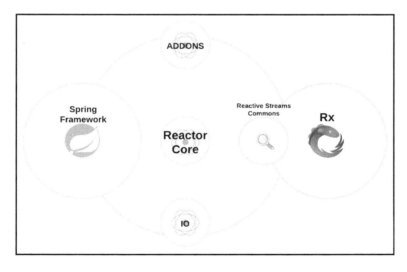

Figure 5: Spring Framework + Reactor + Rx

Reactor is Pivotal's (**SpringSource**) answer to implementing Reactive Streams Specification. As mentioned earlier, Spring is heavily invested in Reactor and this section aims to delve a bit deeper into Reactor.

Reactor is a fourth-generation reactive library for building non-blocking applications on the JVM based on the Reactive Streams Specification.

An overview of the history of **Project Reactor** can be pictorially represented in the following figure:

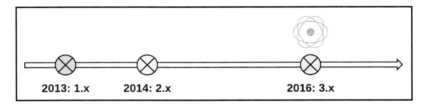

Figure 6: Project Reactor history

The figure above shows the major releases of Project Reactor. The project kick started in the year 2013 (1.x version) and the major release of 3.x was released in the year 2016. As of writing this book, the core module of the framework is at version 3.1.8.RELEASE.

Now that we have a brief understanding of Spring Framework and its connection with reactive programming, lets dive a bit deep into Project Reactor.

Modules in Reactor

With the latest release of Reactor 3.0 the project has been structured with modularity in mind. Reactor 3.0 consists of four major components namely Core, IO, Addons, and Reactive Streams Commons.

- **Reactor Core** (https://github.com/reactor/reactor-core): The main library within Reactor. It provides foundational, non-blocking JVM-compliant Reactive Streams Specification implementations. It also contains code for Reactor types, such as Flux and Mono.
- **Reactor IO** (https://github.com/reactor/reactor-ipc): It contains backpressure-ready components that can be used to encode, decode, send (unicast, multicast, or request/response), and then serve connections. It also contains support for **Kafka** (https://kafka.apache.org/), **Netty** (http://netty.io/), and **Aeron** (https://github.com/real-logic/aeron).

- **Addons** (https://github.com/reactor/reactor-addons): As the name suggests, these are add-ons that consist of three components:
  - reactor-adapter: Contains a bridge to RxJava 1 or 2 types, such as Observable, Completable, Single, Maybe, and Mono/Flux back and forth.
  - reactor-logback: Supports logback over asynchronous reactor-core processors.
  - reactor-extra: Contains more operations for Flux, which include mathematical operations such as sum and average.
- **Reactive Streams Commons** (https://github.com/reactor/reactive-streams-commons): A collaboration experiment project between Spring's Reactor and RxJava. It also contains Reactor-Streams-compliant operators that both projects implement. Issues fixed on one project are also fixed on the other.

Reactive types in Reactor Core

Reactor provided two reactive types, Flux and Mono, that implement Rx extensively. They can be represented as a timeline in which elements are sequenced according to how they arrived. It is important that you get the hang of these two types. Let's do that in the following subsections.

The Flux reative type

A Reactive Streams publisher with Rx operators that emits *0* to *N* elements, and then completes (successfully or with an error). For more information, you can check the following link: https://projectreactor.io

Flux<T> is a Publisher<T> with basic flow operations and supports *0..n* elements.

The definition of Flux is as follows:

```
public abstract class Flux<T>
  extends Object
  implements Publisher<T>
```

The following figure, as depicted in the `Flux` documentation, explains the working of `Flux` in more detail:

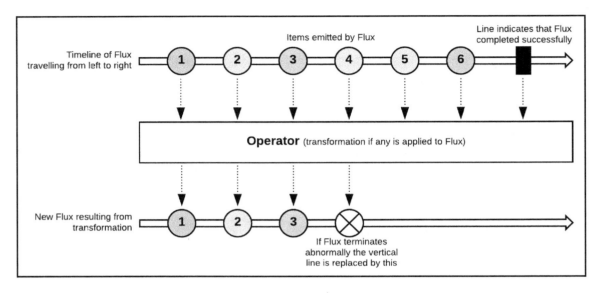

Figure 7: Working of Flux

Flux support is in Spring 5 and a variety of other important modules, including Spring Security. Operators acting on `Flux` would create new publishers.

Please refer to the Reactor Flux documentation for more information: `https://projectreactor.io/docs/core/release/api/reactor/core/publisher/Flux.html`.

Now, let's have a look at some code examples where usage of `Flux` is shown:

- Creating empty `Flux`:

```
Flux<String> emptyFlux = Flux.empty();
```

- Creating `Flux` with items in it:

```
Flux<String> itemFlux = Flux.just("Spring", "Security", "Reactive");
```

- Creating `Flux` from an existing list:

```
List<String> existingList = Arrays.asList("Spring", "Security",
"Reactive");
Flux<String> listFlux = Flux.fromIterable(existingList);
```

- Creating `Flux` that emits every x milliseconds in an infinite manner:

```
Flux<Long> timer = Flux.interval(Duration.ofMillis(x));
```

- Creating `Flux` that emits an exception:

```
Flux.error(new CreatedException());
```

The Mono reactive type

A Reactive Streams Publisher with basic Rx operators that completes successfully by emitting an element, or with an error.

– Mcr o JavaDoc

`Mono<T>` is a `Publisher<T>` that supports *0..1* elements.

The definition of `Mono` is as follows:

```
public abstract class Mono<T>
    extends Object
    implements Publisher<T>
```

As detailed in the documentation, the following figure shows the workings of `Mono`:

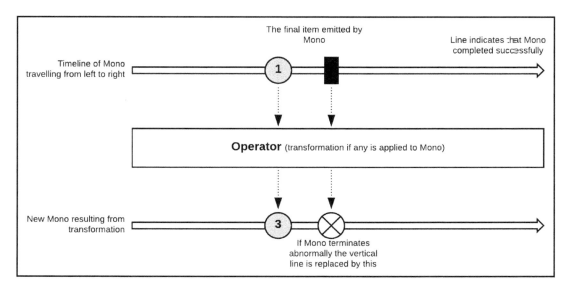

Figure 08: Working of Mono

`Mono<Void>` should be used for a `Publisher` that completes with no value. The documentation explains each method and how it works using a marble diagram, which is self-explanatory. Again, this type is also supported by Spring 5 and Spring Security.

JavaDoc for `Mono` contains more information: `https://projectreactor.io/docs/core/release/api/reactor/core/publisher/Mono.html`.

Let's have a look at some examples:

- Creating empty `Mono`:

    ```
    Mono<String> emptyMono = Mono.empty();
    ```

- Creating `Mono` with a value in it:

    ```
    Mono<String> itemMono = Mono.just("Spring Security Reactive");
    ```

- Creating `Mono` that emits an exception:

    ```
    Mono.error(new CreatedException());
    ```

Data stream types

Broadly, data streams can be categorized into two types:

- **Cold data streams**: There are a number of names by which this is known, such as **Cold Source**, **Cold Observable**, and **Cold Publisher**. These emit data only when one subscribes to it and because of this, all messages produced from start are delivered to the subscriber. If a new `Subscriber` connects to it, the messages are replayed in ascending order and this is same for any new `Subscriber`. The `Subscriber` also has a provision to dictate the rate at which the `Publisher` should emit messages. These data streams are good candidates for applying reactive backpressure (`request(n)`), for example, a database cursor or file stream (reading a file).
- **Hot data streams**: Again, this has a number of different names, such as **Hot Source**, **Hot Observable**, and **Hot Publisher**. These emit data irrespective of any subscribers connected. When a new `Subscriber` connects, it just emits the messages from that point in time and cannot replay messages from the start. These cannot pause message emissions, so an alternate mechanism is required to control flow, such as a buffer. Examples of this stream include mouse events and stock prices.

It's important to note that operators on a stream can change their property, going from cold to hot and vice versa. Also, there are times when a merge between hot and cold can happen and their properties change.

Reactor and RxJava

One of the main aspects between the two is RxJava 2.x which is Java 6+ compatible, but Reactor is Java 8+ compatible. If you are going with Spring 5, I urge you to use a Reactor. If you are comfortable with RxJava 2.x, there is no need to migrate to Reactor. Reactor is an implementation of the Reactive Streams Specification, so you can remain agnostic of what the underlying implementation is.

Reactive Web Application

Spring 5 has brought reactive concepts into the world of web application development with the inclusion of a number of important components. Let's cover them here.

Spring WebFlux

Spring 5 has a reactive stack baked into it, using which, web applications can be built on top of Reactive Streams capable of running on new non-blocking servers, such as Netty, Undertow, and Servlet containers, running on Servlet specifications greater than 3.1.

Existing web application frameworks, such as Spring MVC, are built for Servlet containers from the outset, but Spring 5 brings with it a new web application framework, Spring WebFlux, created with reactive in mind. We have a dedicated chapter in this book covering Spring WebFlux (`Chapter 5`, *Integrating with Spring WebFlux*), so I won't be delving deep into this here. It's good to know that Spring 5 has serious thoughts on reactive and that it is reflected clearly in all these new additions.

Spring WebFlux requires Reactor to be included as one of its core dependencies. But, as always, it does allow you to switch implementations quite easily, if needs be.

Reactive Spring Web

The **Spring Web Module** (`https://github.com/spring-projects/spring-framework/tree/master/spring-web`) has many foundational pieces used to build reactive web applications. It allows you to do operations pertaining to the server and the client.

The capabilities that it provides on the server are divided into two areas:

- **HTTP**: Contained within the `org.springframework.http` package in `spring-web` and contains various APIs for HTTP request handling for supported servers
- **Web**: Contained within the `org.springframework.web` package in `spring-web` and contains various APIs for request processing

This module also contains message codecs that work on the client and aid in encoding and decoding requests and responses. These codecs can also be used on the server.

WebClient

The interface `org.springframework.web.reactive.function.client.WebClient` is a reactive web client introduced in Spring 5 that can be used to perform web requests. Similarly there is `org.springframework.test.web.reactive.server.WebTestClient` interface, which is a special `WebClient`—used to write unit tests within your application. `WebClient` is the reactive version of `RestTemplate`, which works over the HTTP/1.1 protocol. They are packaged as part of the `spring-webflux` module.

WebSockets

The `spring-webflux` module also has reactive WebSocket implementation. **WebSocket** allows us to establish a two-way connection between the client and server, and usage of this is becoming more mainstream in new-generation applications.

Application security

Application security is composed of various processes put in place to find, fix, and prevent security vulnerabilities in an application.

We are living in the world of **Development + Operations** (**DevOps**) where we bring engineering and operational staff together. DevOps advocates automation and monitoring at all levels. With security becoming a very important consideration, a new term, **DevSecOps**, is becoming prominent—this is where we bring in security as a first-class citizen.

For an application, security comes under the nonfunctional requirements. Due to its importance in an application, most organizations have dedicated teams that test applications for potential security flaws. It's a very important aspect to be considered, as in this modern world, a security breach can seriously ruin an organization's brand.

Security is a very broad term and encompasses many aspects. In this book, we will look at some of the fundamental security concerns using the Spring Framework module—Spring Security. After covering some of the core security concerns, we will also look at some of the low-level security problems and how Spring Security can help deal with them.

Since we will be focusing on Spring, we will be delving deep into security concerns with respect to a Java web application development.

Spring Security

Spring Security is a powerful and highly customizable authentication and access-control framework. It is the de facto standard for securing Spring-based applications.

– Spring by Pivotal

Spring Security 5 is the new version of the framework and will be the main focus of this book. Spring Security enables you to take care of authentication and authorization of your application in all aspects. It also has top-level projects to deal specifically with a number of authentication mechanisms, such as **LDAP, OAuth**, and **SAML**. Spring Security also gives you enough mechanisms to deal with common security attacks, such as **Session Fixation, Clickjacking**, and **Cross-Site Request Forgery**. Moreover, it has very good integration with a number of Spring Framework projects, such as Spring MVC, Spring WebFlux, Spring Data, Spring Integration, and Spring Boot.

Spring Security terminologies

It's important to understand some of the most important Spring Security terminologies. Let's look at some of them:

- **Principal**: Any user, device, or system (application) that would like to interact with your application.
- **Authentication**: A process by which your application makes sure that the principal is who they claim to be.

- **Credentials**: When a principal tries to interact with your application, the authentication process kicks in and challenges the principal to pass on some values. One such example is a username/password combination and these values are called credentials. The authentication process validates the principal's passed-in credentials against a data store and replies back with the appropriate result.
- **Authorization**: After successful authentication, the principal is checked again for actions that it can perform on your application. This process of checking rights for a principal and then granting necessary permissions is called authorization.
- **Secured item/resource**: The item or resource that is marked as secured and requires the principal (user) to successfully complete both authentication and authorization.
- **GrantedAuthority**: A Spring Security object (`org.springframework.security.core.GrantedAuthority` interface) that contains/holds permissions/access-right details of a principal.
- **SecurityContext**: A Spring Security object that holds a principal's authentication details.

Spring Security's core features

Spring Security provides a number of security features for your application. The two main features for which Spring Security is well-known are it's **support for a variety of authentication** and **authorization methodologies**. In this section, we will delve deeply into these core features in more detail.

Authentication

Spring Security provides a number of approaches by which your application can authenticate. It also allows you to write a custom authentication mechanism if these provided default approaches don't fit your requirements. Because of this extensibility, you can even use the legacy application against which authentication can be done. The book has a dedicated chapters (Chapter 3, *Authentication Using SAML, LDAP, and OAuth/OIDC* and Chapter 4, *Authentication Using CAS and JAAS*) where we will cover various authentications mechanisms, such as OAuth, LDAP, and SAML, in more detail.

Authorization

Spring Security allows you, as an application developer, many choices by which you can authorize user's access to various parts of your application. Here are some of the approaches:

- **Web URL**: Based on a URL or URL pattern, you can control access
- **Method invocation**: Even a method in a Java Bean can be access-control ed if needs be
- **Domain instance**: One of the very cool features is to control access to specific data by having access control of certain needed domain objects within your application
- **Web service**: Allows you to secure exposed web services in your application

In the next chapter, we will get into these aspects in a bit more detail with more code snippets.

Spring Security 5's new features

Spring Security 5 provides a number of new features along with support for Spring 5. Some of the important new features introduced as part of this release are:

- **Support for OAuth 2.0 and OpenID Connect (OIDC) 1.0**: Allows users to log in to your application using their existing OAuth provider (for example, GitHub) or OIDC provider (for example, Google). OAuth is implemented using Authorization Code Flow. We will delve deep into this in subsequent chapters.
- **Reactive support**: Spring 5 introduced a new reactive web application framework—Spring WebFlux. Spring Security made sure that this web application framework is fully supported in all aspects (authentication and authorization) using reactive concepts.
- **Improved password encoding**: The introduction of the password-encoding delegation allows usage of more than one algorithm for encoding various passwords. The way Spring identifies the algorithm is by reading the prefix of the encoded password, which contains the algorithm used to encode the password. The format is `{algorithm}encoded_password`.

Working of Spring Security

In this section, we will look at how Spring Security works. We will first explain the core concepts and then look at various classes the request goes through to perform security.

Servlet Filter

It's quite important to understand Servlet Filter so you can understand Spring Security internals. The following figure clearly explains a Servlet Filter in action. It comes before the request reaches the actual resource and also before the response if sent back to the consumer. It's a pluggable component that can be introduced at any time with configuration in the web configuration file (`web.xml`).

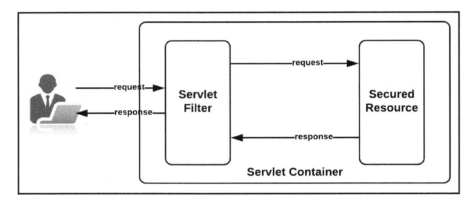

Figure 9: Working of Servlet Filter

Filter Chain

You can embed any number of Servlet Filters before they reach the actual resource. The filters are fired according to the order in which they are declared in `web.xml`. This chaining of the Servlet Filter is called **Filter Chain**. Spring Security works on a number of Servlet Filters arranged as a Filter Chain, each filter performing a single responsibility, then handing it over to the next one, and so on. Most of the built-in filters are good enough for most applications. If needs be, you can write your own filters and place them wherever you want them to be executed.

Security Interceptor (DelegatingFilterProxy)

When any request reaches an application that is secured using Spring Security, there is a gate the request goes through. This interceptor does all the magic and if things don't look good, it errors out and goes back to the caller, as shown in the following figure:

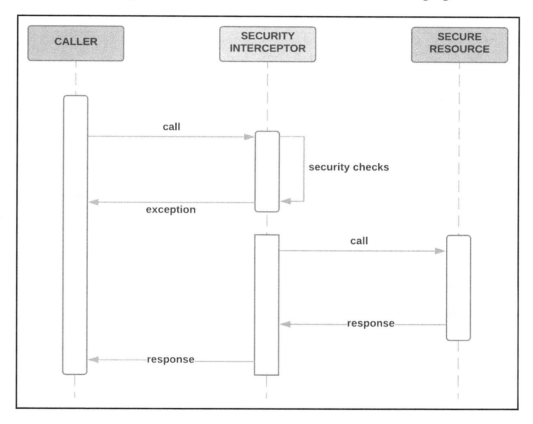

Figure 10: Working of Security Interceptor

The Security Interceptor makes sure that, according to various security configurations set up for your application, it delegates the work to appropriate parties and makes sure that everyone is happy before actually reaching the resource requested by the caller. To do the actual job, the Security Interceptor employs a number of managers, each entrusted to do a single job. The following figure lists some of the important managers the Security Interceptor works with to perform the function:

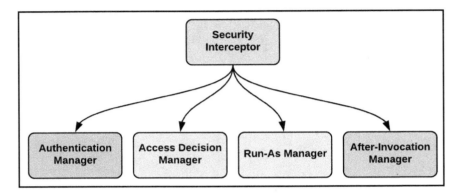

Figure 11: Security Interceptor and associated managers

In Spring Security, the Security Interceptor is accomplished by `DelegatingFilterProxy`. For any request that reaches the web application, this proxy makes sure to delegate the request to Spring Security, and when things go well, it makes sure that the request is taken to the right resource within the web application.

`DelegatingFilterProxy` is a Servlet Filter that has to be configured in your `web.xml` file, which then delegates to a Spring-managed bean (`@Bean`) that implements a `ServletFilter` interface.

The following code snippet shows how to configure `DelegatingProxyFilter` in `web.xml`:

```xml
<?xml version="1.0" encoding="UTF-8"?>
<web-app>
   <filter>
      <filter-name>springSecurityFilterChain</filter-name>
      <filter-class>
         org.springframework.web.filter.DelegatingFilterProxy
      </filter-class>
   </filter>

   <filter-mapping>
      <filter-name>springSecurityFilterChain</filter-name>
```

```
            <url-pattern>/*</url-pattern>
        </filter-mapping>
    </web-app>
```

In the preceding code, all the requests to the web application (`/*` mapping) would go through the `DelegatingProxyFilter` filter. It's important to note that the name of this filter should be `springSecurityFilterChain` as Spring Security looks for this default filter name to configure itself. The proxy filter just passes/delegates the control to a bean named `springSecuirtyFilterChain`. If you are using the default Spring Security setup, the request would then be received by `FilterChainProxy`. `FilterChainProxy` is responsible for passing the request through the various Servlet Filters configured as part of Spring Security. The `springSecuirtyFilterChain` bean need not be explicitly declared, instead, it is taken care of by the framework which is transparent to the developer.

Now that we've looked at all the core concepts of Spring Security, let's come back to the working of Spring Security as pictorially represented in the following diagram. It contains two important security aspects –Authentication and Authorization:

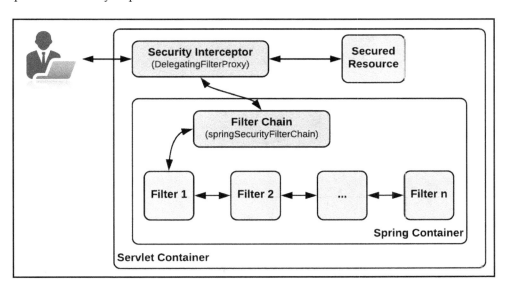

Figure 12: Working of Spring Security

The request from the caller reaches `DelegatingFilterProxy`, which delegates to `FilterChainProxy` (Spring Bean), which in turn passes the request through a number of filters, and after successful execution, grants access to the secured resource the caller has asked for.

For the complete list of Servlet Filters and their functions, I urge you to go through the Spring Security reference: `https://docs.spring.io/spring-security/site/docs/current/reference/html/security-filter-chain.html`.

With all these details, the following figure sums up how Spring Security takes care of Authentication and Authorization for your web application:

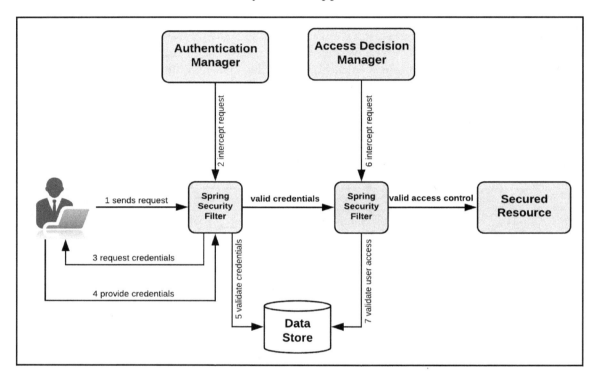

Figure 13: Authentication and Authorization in Spring Security using a database

When a caller sends a request to a web application protected by Spring Security, it first goes through the Security Interceptor managers, such as **Authentication Manager** (responsible for authentication) and **Access Decision Manager** (responsible for authorization), and after executing these successfully, gives the caller access to the secured resource.

For reactive applications, these concepts are all valid. There are equivalent reactive classes and the way we code is the only thing that changes. These are easy to understand and implement.

In Chapter 2, *Deep Diving into Spring Security*, we will cover Authentication, and in Chapter 3, *Authentication Using SAML, LDAP, and OAuth/OIDC*, we will cover Authorization in detail and delve a bit more deeply into its internals.

Core Spring Security modules

In Spring Framework, Spring Security is a top-level project. Within the Spring Security project (https://github.com/spring-projects/spring-security), there are a number of sub-modules:

- **Core** (spring-security-core): Spring security's core classes and interfaces on authentication and access control reside here.
- **Remoting** (spring-security-remoting): In case you need Spring Remoting, this is the module with the necessary classes.
- **Aspect** (spring-security-aspects): **Aspect-Oriented Programming (AOP)** support within Spring Security.
- **Config** (spring-security-config): Provides XML and Java configuration support.
- **Crypto** (spring-security-crypto): Contains cryptography support.
- **Data** (spring-security-data): Integration with Spring Data.
- **Messaging** (spring-security-messaging)
- **OAuth2**: Support for OAuth 2.x support within Spring Security:
  - **Core** (spring-security-oauth2-core)
  - **Client** (spring-security-oauth2-client)
  - **JOSE** (spring-security-oauth2-jose)
- **OpenID** (spring-security-openid): OpenID web-authentication support.
- **CAS** (spring-security-cas): CAS (Central Authentication Service) client integration.
- **TagLib** (spring-security-taglibs): Various tag libraries regarding Spring Security.
- **Test** (spring-security-test): Testing support.
- **Web** (spring-security-web): Contains web security infrastructure code, such as various filters and other Servlet API dependencies.

These are the top-level projects within Spring Framework that are strongly linked to Spring Security:

- `spring-ldap`: Simplifying **Lightweight Directory Access Protocol (LDAP)** programming in Java.
- `spring-security-oauth`: Easy programming with OAuth 1.x and OAuth 2.x protocols.
- `spring-security-saml`: Bringing the SAML 2.0 service provider capabilities to Spring applications.
- `spring-security-kerberos`: Bringing easy integration of Spring application with Kerberos protocol.

Security Assertion Markup Language (SAML) is an XML-based framework for ensuring that transmitted communications are secure. SAML defines mechanisms to exchange authentication, authorization, and non-repudiation information, allowing single sign-on capabilities for Web services.

The **Lightweight Directory Access Protocol (LDAP)** is a directory service protocol that runs on a layer above the TCP/IP stack. Its based on a client-server model and provides a mechanism used to connect to, search, and modify Internet directories.

Kerberos is a network authentication protocol. It is designed to provide strong authentication for client/server applications by using secret key cryptography. A free implementation of this protocol is available from MIT and it is also available in many commercial products.

For more information about SAML, LDAP, and Kerberos, you can check the following links:

- https://www.webopedia.com/TERM/S/SAML.html
- https://msdn.microsoft.com/en-us/library/aa367008(v=vs.85).aspx
- https://web.mit.edu/kerberos/

Summary

In this chapter, we introduced you to new application requirements and then moved to some of the core reactive concepts. We looked at the Reactive Manifesto and reactive programming. We then moved our attention to Spring 5 and Spring Security 5, and touched on some of the new features in it, especially regarding reactive programming. We then looked briefly at Spring's reactive programming efforts by introducing you to Project Reactor. After that, we explored Spring Security in a bit more detail to refresh your thoughts on this subject. Finally, we closed this chapter by giving you an idea of how examples would be structured in this book and what coding practices we will be using.

You should now have a good grasp on reactive programming, and on Spring Security and how it works. You should also have a clear understanding of how to go through the rest of the chapters, especially the example code.

2

Deep Diving into Spring Security

This is a hands-on book, but our first chapter was theoretical (as it should be) because it was an introductory chapter.

In this chapter, we will dive deeply into the technical capabilities of Spring Security, specifically authentication and authorization, using code. However, before we get into the coding, we will give a brief explanation of the theory. We are doing this because it is important to understand the concepts before diving into coding.

The two most important aspects of security are as follows:

- Find the identity of the user
- Find what resources this user has access to

authentication is the mechanism by which you find out who a user is, and authorization is the mechanism that allows an application to find out what the user can do with the application:

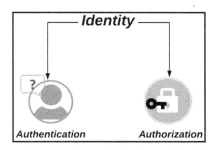

Figure 01: Fundamental aspects of security—Authentication and Authorization

In this chapter we will cover the following:

- Authentication
- Authentication mechanisms
- Authorization

Authentication

One of the fundamental ways to secure a resource is to make sure that the caller is who they claim to be. This process of checking credentials and making sure that they are genuine is called **authentication**.

The following diagram shows the fundamental process Spring Security uses to address this core security requirement. The figure is generic and can be used to explain all the various authentication methods that the framework supports:

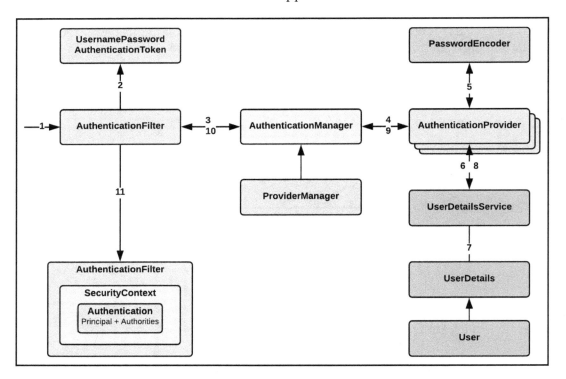

Figure 02: Authentication architecture

As detailed in Chapter 1, *Overview of Spring 5 and Spring Security 5* (in the *Working of Spring Security* section), Spring Security has a series of servlet filters (a filter chain). When a request reaches the server, it is intercepted by this series of filters (*Step 1* in the preceding diagram).

In the reactive world (with the new Spring WebFlux web application framework), filters are written quite differently than traditional filters (such as those used in the Spring MVC web application framework). Having said that, the fundamental mechanism remains the same for both. We have a dedicated chapter explaining how to convert a Spring Security application to Spring MVC and Spring WebFlux where we will cover these aspects in a bit more detail.

The Servlet filter code execution in the filter chain keeps skipping until the right filter is reached. Once it reaches the right authentication filter based on the authentication mechanism used, it extracts the supplied credentials (most commonly a username and password) from the caller. Using the supplied values (here, we have a username and password), the filter (UsernamePasswordAuthenticationFilter) creates an Authentication object (in the preceding diagram, UsernamePasswordAuthenticationToken is created using the username and password supplied in *Step 2*). The Authentication object created in *Step 2* is then used to call the authenticate method in theAuthenticationManager interface:

```
public interface AuthenticationManager {
    Authentication authenticate(Authentication authentication)
        throws AuthenticationException;
}
```

The actual implementation is provided by *ProviderManager*, which has a list of configured AuthenticationProvider.

```
public interface AuthenticationProvider {
    Authentication authenticate(Authentication authentication)
        throws AuthenticationException;
    boolean supports(Class<?> authentication);
}
```

The request passes through various providers and, in due course, tries to authenticate the request. There are a number of AuthenticationProvider as part of Spring Security.

In the diagram at the start of the chapter, AuthenticationProvider requires user details (some providers require this, but some don't), which are provided in UserDetailsService:

```
public interface UserDetailsService {
    UserDetails loadUserByUsername(String username) throws
        UsernameNotFoundException;
}
```

UserDetailsService retrieves UserDetails (and implements the User interface) using the supplied username.

If all goes well, Spring Security creates a fully populated Authentication object (authenticate: true, granted authority list and username), which will contain various necessary details. The Authentication object is stored in the SecurityContext object by the filter for future use.

The authenticate method in AuthenticationManager can return the following:

- An Authentication object with authenticated=true, if Spring Security can validate the supplied user credentials
- An AuthenticationException, if Spring Security finds that the supplied user credentials are invalid
- null, if Spring Security cannot decide whether it is true or false (confused state)

Setting up AuthenticationManager

There are number of built-in AuthenticationManager in Spring Security that can be easily used in your application. Spring Security also has a number of helper classes, using which you can set up AuthenticationManager. One helper class is AuthenticationManagerBuilder. Using this class, its quite easy to set up UserDetailsService against a database, in memory, in LDAP, and so on. If the need arises, you could also have your own custom UserDetailsService (maybe a custom single sign-on solution is already there in your organization).

You can make an `AuthenticationManager` global, so it will be accessible by your entire application. It will be available for method security and other `WebSecurityConfigurerAdapter` instances. `WebSecurityConfigurerAdapter` is a class that is extended by your Spring configuration file, making it quite easy to bring Spring Security into your Spring application. This is how you set up a global `AuthenticationManager` using the `@Autowired` annotation:

```
@Configuration
@EnableWebSecurity
public class SpringSecurityConfig extends WebSecurityConfigurerAdapter {
    @Autowired
    public void confGlobalAuthManager(AuthenticationManagerBuilder auth)
throws
            Exception {
        auth
            .inMemoryAuthentication()
.withUser("admin").password("admin@password").roles("ROLE_ADMIN");
    }
}
```

You can also create local `AuthenticationManager`, which is only available for this particular `WebSecurityConfigurerAdapter`, by overriding the `configure` method, as shown in the following code:

```
@Configuration
@EnableWebSecurity
public class SpringSecurityConfig extends WebSecurityConfigurerAdapter {
    @Override
    protected void configure(AuthenticationManagerBuilder auth) throws
Exception {
        auth
            .inMemoryAuthentication()
.withUser("admin").password("admin@password").roles("ROLE_ADMIN");
    }
}
```

Another option is to expose the `AuthenticationManager` bean by overriding `authenticationManagerBean` method, as shown here:

```
@Override
    public AuthenticationManager authenticationManagerBean() throws
Exception {
        return super.authenticationManagerBean();
    }
```

You can also expose various `AuthenticationManager`, `AuthenticationProvider`, or `UserDetailsService` as beans which will override the default ones.

In the preceding code examples we have used `AuthenticationManagerBuilder` to configure in-memory authentication. More mechanisms of the `AuthenticationManagerBuilder` class will be used in the subsequent examples in this chapter.

AuthenticationProvider

`AuthenticationProvider` provides a mechanism for getting user details, with which authentication can be performed. Spring Security provides a number of `AuthenticationProvider` implementations, as shown in the following diagram:

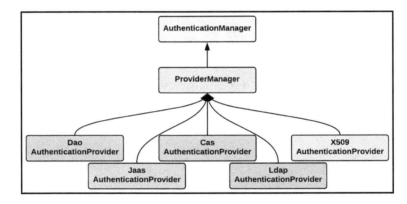

Figure 03: Spring Security built-in AuthenticationProvider

In subsequent chapters, we will go through each of these in detail with more code samples.

Custom AuthenticationProvider

If needs be, we can write a custom `AuthenticationProvider` by implementing the `AuthenticationProvider` interface. We will have to implement two methods, namely `authenticate(Authentication)` and `supports(Class<?> aClass)`:

```
@Component
public class CustomAuthenticationProvider implements
AuthenticationProvider {
    @Override
```

```
         public Authentication authenticate(Authentication authentication)
throws
               AuthenticationException {
         String username = authentication.getName();
         String password = authentication.getCredentials().toString();
         if ("user".equals(username) && "password".equals(password)) {
            return new UsernamePasswordAuthenticationToken
              (username, password, Collections.emptyList());
         } else {
            throw new BadCredentialsException("Authentication failed");
         }
      }
      @Override
      public boolean supports(Class<?> aClass) {
         return aClass.equals(UsernamePasswordAuthenticationToken.class);
      }
   }
```

Our `authenticate` method is quite simple. We just compare the username and password with a static value. We can write any logic here and authenticate the user. If there is an error, it throws an exception, `AuthenticationException`.

On the book's GitHub page, navigate to the `jetty-in-memory-basic-custom-authentication` project to see the full source code of this class.

Multiple AuthenticationProvider

Spring Security allows you to declare multiple `AuthenticationProvider` in your application. They are executed according to the order in which they are declared in the configuration.

The `jetty-in-memory-basic-custom-authentication` project is modified further, and we have used the newly created `CustomAuthenticationProvider` as an `AuthenticationProvider` (Order 1) and the existing `inMemoryAuthentication` as our second `AuthenticationProvider` (Order 2):

```
@EnableWebSecurity
@ComponentScan(basePackageClasses = CustomAuthenticationProvider.class)
public class SpringSecurityConfig extends WebSecurityConfigurerAdapter {

   @Autowired
   CustomAuthenticationProvider customAuthenticationProvider;

   @Override
   protected void configure(HttpSecurity http) throws Exception {
```

```
        http.httpBasic()
                .and()
                .authorizeRequests()
                .antMatchers("/**")
                .authenticated(); // Use Basic authentication
    }
    @Override
    protected void configure(AuthenticationManagerBuilder auth) throws
Exception {
        // Custom authentication provider - Order 1
        auth.authenticationProvider(customAuthenticationProvider);
        // Built-in authentication provider - Order 2
        auth.inMemoryAuthentication()
                .withUser("admin")
                .password("{noop}admin@password")
                //{noop} makes sure that the password encoder doesn't do
anything
                .roles("ADMIN") // Role of the user
                .and()
                .withUser("user")
                .password("{noop}user@password")
                .credentialsExpired(true)
                .accountExpired(true)
                .accountLocked(true)
                .roles("USER");
    }
}
```

Whenever the `authenticate` method executes without error, the controls return and thereafter configured `AuthenticationProvider`'s doesn't get executed.

Sample application

Let's gets our hands dirty by doing some coding. We will start off with the most common authentication mechanisms and then get into other authentication mechanisms that can be used with Spring Security.

Base project setup

Apart from the actual authentication mechanism, many aspects of the application are quite similar. In this section, we will set up the example and then cover the specific authentication mechanism in detail.

We will be using the default Spring Security DB schema against which we will authenticate the user. We will create a fully fledged Spring MVC web application, with each component being created from scratch. Creating a sample Spring Security application using Spring MVC with the help of Spring Boot is very easy. The application will function through many things that are hidden away from developers. But in this case, we will be creating this application component by component so that you can see the actual code with which a web application that is built on Spring MVC can be secured.

The default DB schema used by Spring Security is shown in the following diagram. However, you can customize it the way you think it is suitable for your application. We will be using the **Users** and **Authorities** tables for our setup here:

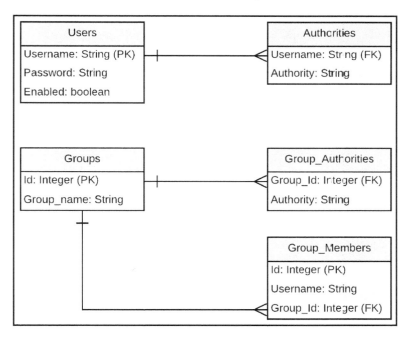

Figure 04: Spring Security default database schema

Let's now start developing our sample application.

Step 1—Create a Maven project in IntelliJ IDEA

In IntelliJ, select **File | New | Project**. This will open up the **New Project** wizard, as shown in the following screenshot. Now select **Maven** and click the **Next** button:

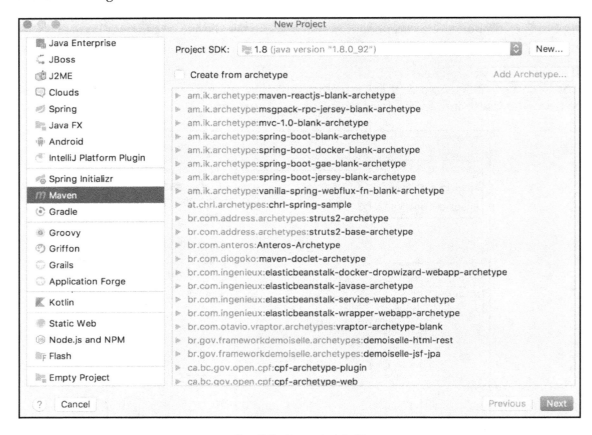

Figure 05: New Maven project in IntelliJ

On the next screen in the **New Project** wizard (*Step 2*), enter the **GroupId**, **ArtifactId**, and **Version**, as shown in the following screenshot:

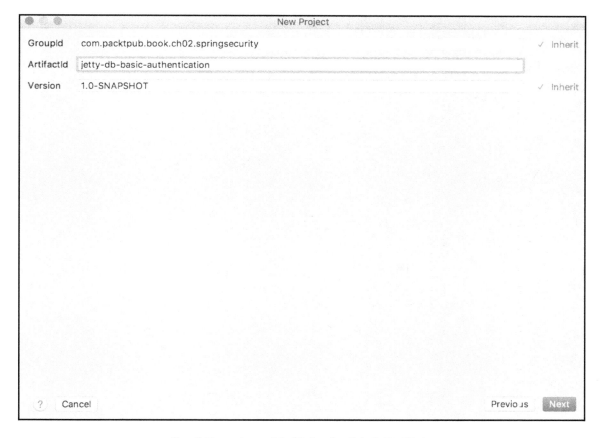

Figure 06: Maven project setup in IntelliJ—Input GroupId, ArtifactId and Version

On the next screen in the **New Project** wizard (*Step 3*), enter the **Project name** and **Project location**, as shown in the following screenshot:

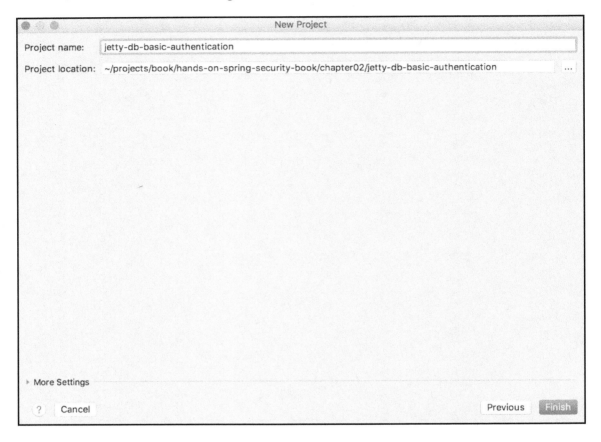

Figure 07: Maven project setup—Setting Project name and Project location

IntelliJ will prompt you with instructions, as shown in the following screenshot. To automatically import projects whenever you make any changes in `pom.xml`, click on the **Enable Auto-Import** link:

Figure 08: Enabling Auto-Import in IntelliJ

Step 2—pom.xml changes

Open the `pom.xml` file and add the following code within the project tag
(`<project></project>`):

```xml
<!-- Spring dependencies -->
<dependency>
    <groupId>org.springframework.security</groupId>
    <artifactId>spring-security-web</artifactId>
    <version>5.0.4.RELEASE</version>
</dependency>
<dependency>
    <groupId>org.springframework.security</groupId>
    <artifactId>spring-security-config</artifactId>
    <version>5.0.4.RELEASE</version>
</dependency>
<dependency>
    <groupId>org.springframework.security</groupId>
    <artifactId>spring-security-crypto</artifactId>
    <version>5.0.4.RELEASE</version>
</dependency>
<dependency>
    <groupId>org.springframework</groupId>
    <artifactId>spring-webmvc</artifactId>
    <version>5.0.5.RELEASE</version>
</dependency>
<dependency>
    <groupId>org.springframework</groupId>
    <artifactId>spring-jdbc</artifactId>
    <version>5.0.4.RELEASE</version>
</dependency>
<!-- Servlet and JSP related dependencies -->
<dependency>
    <groupId>javax.servlet</groupId>
    <artifactId>javax.servlet-api</artifactId>
    <version>3.1.0</version>
    <scope>provided</scope>
</dependency>
<dependency>
    <groupId>javax.servlet.jsp</groupId>
    <artifactId>javax.servlet.jsp-api</artifactId>
    <version>2.3.1</version>
    <scope>provided</scope>
</dependency>
<dependency>
    <groupId>javax.servlet.jsp.jstl</groupId>
    <artifactId>javax.servlet.jsp.jstl-api</artifactId>
    <version>1.2.1</version>
```

```
    </dependency>
    <dependency>
        <groupId>taglibs</groupId>
        <artifactId>standard</artifactId>
        <version>1.1.2</version>
    </dependency>
    <!-- For datasource configuration -->
    <dependency>
        <groupId>org.apache.commons</groupId>
        <artifactId>commons-dbcp2</artifactId>
        <version>2.1.1</version>
    </dependency>
    <!-- We will be using MySQL as our database server -->
    <dependency>
        <groupId>mysql</groupId>
        <artifactId>mysql-connector-java</artifactId>
        <version>6.0.6</version>
    </dependency>
```

Build a setup on `pom.xml` in which we will be using jetty to run the application created.

```
<build>
    <plugins>
        <!-- We will be using jetty plugin to test the war file -->
        <plugin>
            <groupId>org.eclipse.jetty</groupId>
            <artifactId>jetty-maven-plugin</artifactId>
            <version>9.4.8.v20171121</version>
        </plugin>
    </plugins>
</build>
```

Step 3—MySQL database schema setup

Create a default database schema using the following scripts, and insert some users:

```
create table users(
    username varchar(75) not null primary key,
    password varchar(150) not null,
    enabled boolean not null
);
create table authorities (
    username varchar(75) not null,
    authority varchar(50) not null,
    constraint fk_authorities_users foreign key(username) references
users(username)
);
```

Insert data into the preceding tables using the following scripts:

```
insert into users(username, password, enabled)
    values('admin',
'$2a$04$1cVPCpEk5DOCCAxOMleFcOJvIiYURH01P9rx1Y/pl.wJpkNTfWO6u', true);
insert into authorities(username, authority)
    values('admin','ROLE_ADMIN');
insert into users(username, password, enabled)
    values('user',
'$2a$04$nbz5hF5uzq3qsjzY8ZLpnueDAvwj4x0U9SVtLPDROk4vpmuHdvG3a', true);
insert into authorities(username,authority)
    values('user','ROLE_USER');
```

The `password` is one-way hashed using online tool `http://www.devglan.com/online-tools/bcrypt-hash-generator`. To compare the `password` we will use `PasswordEncoder` (`Bcrypt`).

Credentials are as follows:

- User = `admin` and password = `admin@password`
- User = `user` and password = `user@password`

 It's important to note that, even though the role is named `ROLE_ADMIN`, the actual name is `ADMIN`, and this is what our code will be using while passing.

Step 4—Setting up MySQL database properties in your project

Create a file named `mysqldb.properties` in the `src/main/resources` folder with the following content:

```
mysql.driver=com.mysql.cj.jdbc.Driver
mysql.jdbcUrl=jdbc:mysql://localhost:3306/spring_security_schema?useSSL=false
mysql.username=root
mysql.password=<your-db-password>
```

Step 5—Spring application configuration

Create a Java class named `ApplicationConfig` with the following code in
the `com.packtpub.book.ch02.springsecurity.config` package:

```
@Configuration
@PropertySource("classpath:mysqldb.properties")
public class ApplicationConfig {

    @Autowired
    private Environment env;

    @Bean
    public DataSource getDataSource() {
        BasicDataSource dataSource = new BasicDataSource();
        dataSource.setDriverClassName(env.getProperty("mysql.driver"));
        dataSource.setUrl(env.getProperty("mysql.jdbcUrl"));
        dataSource.setUsername(env.getProperty("mysql.username"));
        dataSource.setPassword(env.getProperty("mysql.password"));
        return dataSource;
    }
}
```

Step 6—Web application configuration

In this example, we are going to use Spring MVC as our web application framework. Let's
create the web application configuration file:

```
@Configuration
@EnableWebMvc
@ComponentScan(basePackages=
{"com.packtpub.book.ch02.springsecurity.controller"})
public class WebApplicationConfig implements WebMvcConfigurer {
    @Override
    public void configureViewResolvers(ViewResolverRegistry registry) {
        registry.jsp().prefix("/WEB-INF/views/").suffix(".jsp");
    }
}
```

The `@EnableWebMvc` annotation makes sure that your application is based on Spring MVC.

Step 7—Spring MVC setup

In Spring MVC, the request lands on `DispatcherServlet`. `DispatcherServlet` can be declared in `web.xml` or as a Java configuration if your servlet container is 3.0+. Please create a dummy `SpringSecurityConfig.java` file. We will be constructing this class when we explain the first authentication mechanism, namely, basic authentication:

```java
public class SpringMvcWebApplicationInitializer
        extends AbstractAnnotationConfigDispatcherServletInitializer {

    @Override
    protected Class<?>[] getRootConfigClasses() {
        return new Class[] { ApplicationConfig.class,
SpringSecurityConfig.class };
    }

    @Override
    protected Class<?>[] getServletConfigClasses() {
        return new Class[] { WebApplicationConfig.class };
    }

    @Override
    protected String[] getServletMappings() {
        return new String[] { "/" };
    }

}
```

Step 8—Controller setup

Let's create a base controller (`HomeController`) for the secured JSP page (`home.jsp`). Please note that the return of the mapping method should be a string, and it should map to the actual name of the JSP file. In our case, it is `home.jsp`, a secured resource that the caller navigates when they log in:

```java
@Controller
public class HomeController {

    @GetMapping("/")
    public String home(Model model, Principal principal) {
        if(principal != null)
            model.addAttribute("msg", "Welcome " + principal.getName());
        return "home";
    }
}
```

Step 9—JSP creation

Our home page is a very simple JSP file, as shown in the following code snippet. This JSP just displays a message that we have constructed in our `HomeController` class:

```
<%@ page language="java" contentType="text/html; charset=ISO-8859-1"
        pageEncoding="ISO-8859-1"%>
<!DOCTYPE html>
<html>
<head>
    <meta http-equiv="Content-Type" content="text/html; charset=ISO-8859-1">
    <title>Spring Security</title>
</head>
<body>
<h1>Spring Security Sample</h1>
<h2>${msg}</h2>
</body>
</html>
```

This is now the base Spring MVC application, and with this we will try to set up various authentication mechanisms.

Spring Security setup

To explain Spring Security, we will implement basic authentication on the Spring MVC project that we created earlier. In `Chapter 3`, *Authentication Using SAML, LDAP, and OAuth/OIDC*, we will look at implementing other authentication mechanisms using Spring Security. To accomplish basic authentication in your application, let's perform the additional steps outlined in this section.

Step 1—Spring Security configuration setup

We will now create the all-important Spring Security configuration class and make sure that the default filter chain for Spring Security is set up to secure all the resources:

```
@EnableWebSecurity
public class SpringSecurityConfig extends WebSecurityConfigurerAdapter {
    @Autowired
    private DataSource dataSource;
    @Override
    protected void configure(AuthenticationManagerBuilder auth) throws
Exception {
        auth.jdbcAuthentication().dataSource(dataSource)
                .usersByUsernameQuery("select username, password, enabled"
```

```
                            + " from users where username = ?")
                  .authoritiesByUsernameQuery("select username, authority "
                            + "from authorities where username = ?")
                  .passwordEncoder(new BCryptPasswordEncoder());
    }
    @Override
    protected void configure(HttpSecurity http) throws Exception {
        http.authorizeRequests().anyRequest().hasAnyRole('ADMIN', "USER")
                  .and()
                  .httpBasic(); // Use Basic authentication
    }
}
```

In Spring Security configuration, the first thing that we do is tell Spring Security that you will have to authenticate the user against a database by using a defined user query and checking the user's authority using the defined authority query.

We then set up the authentication mechanism to retrieve the user's credentials. Here we are using basic authentication as the mechanism to capture user credentials. Please note that the role names being used to check doesn't have the prefix ROLE_.

Step 2—Spring Security setup for a web application

We know that we have to instruct the application to start using Spring Security. One easy way is to declare the Spring Security filter in web.xml. If you want to avoid using XML and perform the actions using Java instead, then create a class that extends AbstractSecurityWebApplicationInitializer; this will do the trick of initializing the filter and setting Spring Security for your application:

```
public class SecurityWebApplicationInitializer
        extends AbstractSecurityWebApplicationInitializer {

}
```

With this, we have completed all the setup required to see basic authentication in action.

Running the application

Run the project by executing the `mvn jetty:run` command. Once you see the log shown in the following screenshot, open a browser and go to `http://localhost:8080`:

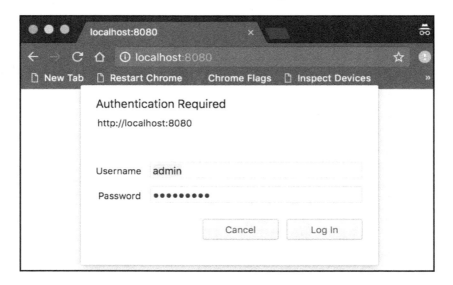

Terminal
```
    INFO: Mapped "{[/],methods=[GET]}" onto public java.lang.String com.packtpub.book.ch02.springsecurity.con
    Apr 16, 2018 9:49:25 PM org.springframework.web.servlet.mvc.method.annotation.RequestMappingHandlerAdapte
    INFO: Looking for @ControllerAdvice: WebApplicationContext for namespace 'dispatcher-servlet': startup da
    Apr 16, 2018 9:49:25 PM org.springframework.web.servlet.DispatcherServlet initServletBean
    INFO: FrameworkServlet 'dispatcher': initialization completed in 487 ms
    [INFO] Started o.e.j.m.p.JettyWebAppContext@622fdb81{/,file:///Users/tjohn/projects/book/spring-security-
    Users/tjohn/projects/book/spring-security-book/chapter02/spring-security-basic-authentication/src/main/we
    [INFO] Started ServerConnector@4cc12db2{HTTP/1.1,[http/1.1]}{0.0.0.0:8080}
    [INFO] Started @7440ms
    [INFO] Started Jetty Server
```

Figure 09: Jetty Server running - console log

Once you access the URL, the browser prompts with a default basic authentication dialog, as shown in the following screenshot. Enter the **Username** and **Password** as `admin/admin@password` and click on **Log In**:

Figure 10: Basic authentication dialog in the browser

If your credentials are correct and if the user has either the ADMIN or USER role, you should see the home page as follows:

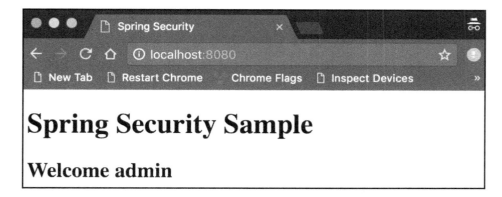

Figure 11: The home page after successful login

 The full project code is available on the book's GitHub page (https://github.com/PacktPublishing/Hands-On-Spring-Security-5-for-Reactive-Applications) within the jetty-db-basic-authentication project.

In-memory user storage

As mentioned earlier, for various testing purposes, it's better to store the user credentials and then authenticate in memory than to use a proper database, such as MySQL. For this, just change the Spring Security configuration file (SpringSecurityConfig.java) by adding the following method:

```
@Override
protected void configure(AuthenticationManagerBuilder auth) throws
Exception {
    auth
.inMemoryAuthentication()
            .withUser("admin")
            .password("{noop}admin@password")
//{noop} makes sure that the password encoder doesn't do anything
            .roles("ADMIN") // Role of the user
            .and()
            .withUser("user")
            .password("{noop}user@password")
            .credentialsExpired(true)
            .accountExpired(true)
```

```
                .accountLocked(true)
                .roles("USER");
    }
```

It's important to note that the password has a prefix, {noop}, attached to it. This ensures that when the password is validated, no encoding is carried out. This is one way to avoid having password encoding errors when you run the project.

 The full source code, as a fully fledged project, can be found on this book's GitHub page in the jetty-in-memory-basic-authentication project.

Run as Spring Boot

The preceding example can be easily converted to a Spring Boot application by following the ensuing additional steps. This process won't cover many of the trivial steps that we have done previously. You need to have one more configuration file, SpringSecurityConfig.java, the details of which are as follows.

You can create a new file, usually named Run.java, with the following code:

```
@SpringBootApplication
public class Run {
    public static void main(String[] args) {
        SpringApplication.run(Run.class, args);
    }
}
```

It's a very simple file with an important annotation in it, @SpringBootApplication. We took away the Spring MVC configuration class and put the following properties in the application.properties file. This is just another way to avoid creating a new Spring MVC configuration file and instead use the properties file:

```
spring.mvc.view.prefix: /WEB-INF/views/
spring.mvc.view.suffix: .jsp
```

As earlier, everything else is kept intact. For the full project, refer to the book's GitHub page in the spring-boot-in-memory-basic-authentication project.

Open a command prompt and enter the following command:

```
mvn spring-boot:run
```

Open the browser and navigate to `http://localhost:8080`, and you should be provided with a basic authentication dialog. After successful login, you should be taken to the user home page, as shown earlier.

Authorization

Once the user is validated in terms of who they claim to be, the next aspect, what the user has access to, needs to be ascertained. This process of making sure what the user is allowed to do within the application is called authorization.

In line with authentication architecture, as seen earlier, authorization also has a manager, `AccessDecisionManager`. Spring Security has three built-in implementations for this: `AffirmativeBased`, `ConsensusBased`, and `UnanimousBased`. `AccessDecisionManager` works by delegating to a chain of `AccessDecisionVoter`. Authorization-related Spring Security classes/interfaces are shown in the following diagram:

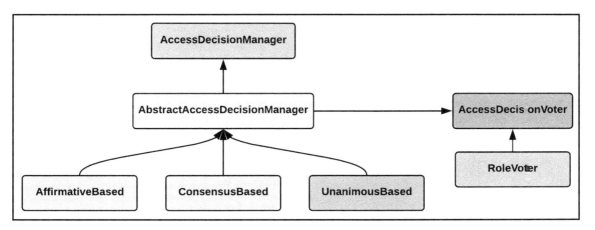

Figure 12: Spring Security Authorization classes/interfaces

In Spring Security, authorization to a secured resource is granted by invoking voters and then tallying the votes received. The three built-in implementations tally the votes received in different manners:

- **AffirmativeBased**: If at least one voter votes, the user is given access to the secured resource
- **ConsensusBased**: If a clear consensus is reached between the voters and their votes, then the user is given access to the secured resource
- **UnanimousBased**: If all the voters vote, then the user is given access to the secured resource

Spring Security provides two authorization approaches:

- **Web URL**: Incoming URL (specific URL or regular expression)-based authorization
- **Method**: Method signature based on which access is controlled

If your serving layer exposes only RESTful endpoints and the data in your application is properly categorized as resources (complying with REST principles), using a Web URL approach can be considered. If your application just exposes endpoints (REST-based, I would call) not really complying with REST principles, you can consider using method-based authorization.

Web URL

Spring Security can be used to set up URL-based authorization. HTTP Security configured can be used with Spring Security configuration to achieve the desired authorization. In many examples that we have gone through so far, we have seen pattern matching authorization. Here is one such example:

- `AntPathRequestMatcher`: Uses an Ant-style pattern for URL matching:

```
http
    .antMatcher("/rest/**")
    .httpBasic()
        .disable()
    .authorizeRequests()
        .antMatchers("/rest/movie/**", "/rest/ticket/**", "/index")
            .hasRole("ROLE_USER");
```

In the preceding code snippet, the `/rest` URL's basic authentication is disabled, and for other URLs (`/rest/movie`, `/rest/ticket` and `/index`), users with the USER role have access. The snippet also shows single match (using `antMatcher`) and multiple matches (using `antMatchers`).

- `MvcRequestMatcher`: This uses Spring MVC to match the path and then extracts variables. The matching is relative to the servlet path.
- `RegexRequestMatcher`: This uses a regular expression to match the URL. It can also be used to match the HTTP method, if needed. The matching is case-sensitive and takes the form (`servletPath` + `pathInfo` + `queryString`):

```
http
    .authorizeRequests()
    .regexMatchers("^((?!(/rest|/advSearch)).)*$").hasRole "ADMIN")
.regexMatchers("^((?!(/rest|/basicSearch)).)*$').access("hasRole(US
ER)")
        .anyRequest()
    .authenticated()
    .and()
    .httpBasic();
```

Method invocation

Spring Security allows users to access-control method execution using **aspect-oriented programming** (**AOP**) in the background. This can be done using XML configuration or using Java configuration. Since we have been following Java configuration throughout this book, we will cover Java configuration and annotations here to explain method security. The best practice is to choose a particular method invocation authorization approach and stick to it for consistency across your application. Choose whichever approach is apt for your application, as there isn't anything particular documented on when to choose what.

If you would like to enable method security in your application, firstly annotate the class with @EnableMethodSecurity. There are three types of annotation with which you can annotate the methods and authorize them. The types are as follows:

- **Voting-based annotations**: the most commonly used annotations in Spring Security. Spring Security's @Secured annotation falls into this category. To use these annotations, they first have to be enabled, as shown in the following code snippet:

```
@Configuration
@EnableGlobalMethodSecurity(securedEnabled = true)
public class SecurityConfig extends WebSecurityConfigurerAdapter {
    // ...
}
```

  Once the usage of annotation is enabled, the @Secured annotation can be used, as shown in the following code snippet:

```
@RestController
@RequestMapping("/movie")
public class MovieController {

    @GetMapping("public")
    @Secured("ROLE_PUBLIC")
    public String publiclyAvailable() {
        return "Hello All!";
    }

    @GetMapping("admin")
    @Secured("ROLE_ADMIN")
    public String adminAccessible() {
        return "Hello Admin!";
    }
}
```

- **JSR-250 security annotations**: This is also called the **Enterprise JavaBeans 3.0 (EJB 3)** security annotation. Again, before using these annotations, they have to be enabled using @EnableGlobalMethodSecurity(jsr250Enabled = true). The following snippet shows the JSR-250 security annotation in action:

```
@RestController
@RequestMapping("/movie")
public class MovieController {

    @GetMapping("public")
    @PermitAll
```

```
        public String publiclyAvailable() {
            return "Hello All!";
        }

        @GetMapping("admin")
        @RolesAllowed({"ROLE_ADMIN"})
        public String adminAccessible() {
            return "Hello Admin!";
        }
    }
```

- **Expression-based annotation**: Annotations based on @Pre and @Post fall into this category. They are enabled using @EnableGlobalMethodSecurity(prePostEnabled = true):

```
    @RestController
    @RequestMapping("/movie")
    public class MovieController {
        @GetMapping("public")
        @PreAuthorize("permitAll()")
        public String publiclyAvailable() {
            return "Hello All!";
        }
        @GetMapping("admin")
        @PreAuthorize("hasAnyAuthority('ROLE_ADMIN')")
        public String adminAccessible() {
            return "Hello Admin!";
        }
    }
```

In the preceding example, hasAnyAuthority is called **Spring Expression Language** (**SpEL**). Similar to the example shown, there are many such predefined expressions that can be used for security.

Domain instance

Spring Security provides ways to access control various permissions attached to any object. Spring Security **Access Control List** (ACL) stores a list of permissions associated with a domain object. It also grants these permissions to various entities that need to perform different operations on the domain object. For Spring Security to work, you need to set up four database tables, as shown in the following diagram:

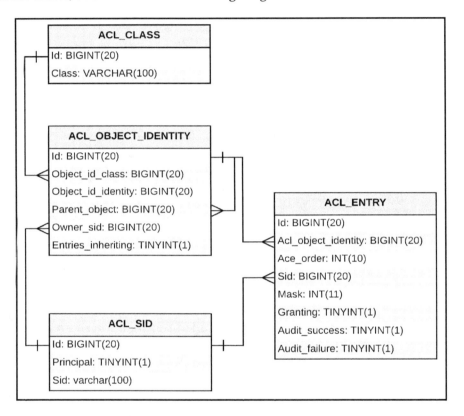

Figure 13: Spring Security ACL database schema

Here is a small explanation of the tables in the preceding diagram:

- ACL_CLASS table: As the name suggests, it stores the domain object's class name.
- ACL_SID table: **Security Identity** (SID) stores either a username (testuser) or role name (ROLE_ADMIN). The PRINCIPAL column stores either 0 or 1, 0 if the SID is a username and 1 if it is a role name.

- `ACL_OBJECT_IDENTITY` table: It is entrusted to store object-related information and links other tables.
- `ACL_ENTRY` table: It stores permission granted to each SID for each `OBJECT_IDENTITY`.

In order for Spring Security ACL to work, it also requires a cache. One of the easiest ones to integrate with Spring is EhCache.

Spring Security ACL supports the following permissions:

- `READ`
- `WRITE`
- `CREATE`
- `DELETE`
- `ADMINISTRATION`

To make it work, we have to enable it using `@EnableGlobalMethodSecurity(prePostEnabled = true, securedEnabled = true)`. We are now ready to put annotations in place to start access controlling domain objects. A code snippet in which Spring ACL is used is as follows:

```
@PostFilter("hasPermission(filterObject, 'READ')")
List<Record> findRecords();
```

After querying for records (post-filtering), the result (a list) is scrutinized, and filtering takes place to only return the object to which the user has `READ` permission. We can also use `@PostAuthorize` as follows:

```
@PostAuthorize("hasPermission(returnObject, 'READ')")
```

After execution of the method (`@Post`), if the user has `READ` access on the object, it is returned. Otherwise, it throws an `AccessDeniedException` exception:

```
@PreAuthorize("hasPermission(#movie, 'WRITE')")
Movie save(@Param("movie")Movie movie);
```

Before the method is fired (`@Pre`), it checks whether the user has the `WRITE` permission on the object. Here, we use the parameter being passed into the method to check for user permission. If the user has permission to `WRITE`, it executes the method. Otherwise, it throws an exception.

We can have a fully fledged example of this, but we are already stretched by the number of topics that this book can cover. So I will leave it just here, and I am sure you now have enough information to make a complete implementation.

Some of the common built-in Spring expressions regarding security are as follows:

Expression	Description
hasRole([role_name])	If the current user has role_name, it returns true
hasAnyRole([role_name1, role_name2])	If the current user has any of the role names in the list, it returns true
hasAuthority([authority])	If the current user has specified authority, it returns true
hasAnyAuthority([authority1, authority2])	If the current user has any of the authorities in the specified list, it returns true
permitAll	Always equates to true
denyAll	Always equates to false
isAnonymous()	If the current user is anonymous, it returns true
isRememberMe()	If the current user has set remember-me, it returns true
isAuthenticated()	If the current user is not anonymous, it returns true
isFullyAuthenticated()	If the current user is not anonymous or remember-me user, it returns true
hasPermission(Object target, Object permission)	If the current user has permission to target object, it returns true
hasPermission(Object targetId, Object targetType, Object permission)	If the current user has permission to target object, it returns true

Other Spring Security capabilities

Spring Security has a number of capabilities apart from core security features, authentication and authorization. Some of the most important ones are listed here. In `Chapter 7`, *Spring Security Add-Ons*, we will go through each of these in more detail using hands-on coding. We will build on the example that we have created in this chapter and explain each of these very important Spring Security capabilities:

- **Remember-me authentication**: This is also known as persistent-login, and it allows websites to remember a user's identity in between multiple sessions. Spring Security provides a couple of implementations (hashed-token-based and persistent-token-based) that make this easy.

- **Cross Site Request Forgery (CSRF)**: This is a very common security exploit employed by hackers to do unethical operations, whereby unauthorized commands are sent on behalf of the user. Spring Security allows us to fix this exploit easily with configurations.

- **Cross-Origin Resource Sharing (CORS)**: This is a mechanism by which a web application running on a particular domain can access resources exposed in another domain by adding additional HTTP headers. This is one of the security mechanisms employed to make sure that only legitimate code can have access to resources exposed by a domain.

- **Session management**: Proper user session management is key to any application's security. Here are some of the important session-related functions that Spring Security takes care of easily:

  - **Session timeout**: This makes sure that user sessions time out at the configured value, and this cannot be hacked.

  - **Concurrent session**: This prevents users from having multiple (configured value) sessions active within the server.

  - **Session fixation**: This is a security attack that allows the attacker to hijack a valid user's session and then start using it for unethical operations.

These are some of the important features that Spring Security brings to the table. We will thoroughly explore them after covering additional topics that are relevant to Spring Security.

Summary

This chapter aimed at introducing two important security concepts, namely authentication and authorization, and how they are supported by Spring Security.

We started by explaining these concepts in detail and then dived into them with the help of a sample application. We have used Spring MVC application as a base to help you understand Spring Security concepts. Chapter 4, *Authentication Using CAS and JAAS*, is aimed at explaining reactive web application framework, Spring WebFlux.

In the next chapter, we will go through other authentication mechanisms supported by Spring Security by extending the example that we have built in this chapter.

3
Authentication Using SAML, LDAP, and OAuth/OIDC

In this chapter, we will look at the authentication mechanisms—namely SAML, LDAP, and OAuth/OIDC—supported by Spring Security. This will be a fully hands-on coding chapter. We will build small applications, most of them starting from the base application that we built in Chapter 2, *Deep Diving into Spring Security*.

The main goal of this chapter is to make you comfortable with implementing the authentication mechanisms most commonly used across your organization, and also to showcase Spring Security module capabilities.

Each of the authentication mechanisms has a project that you can see in the book's GitHub page. However, in the book, we will only cover important aspects of the sample code, to reduce clutter within the chapter.

In this chapter, we will cover the following topics:

- Security Assertion Markup Language
- Lightweight Directory Access Protocol
- OAuth2 and OpenID Connect

Security Assertion Markup Language

Security Assertion Markup Language (SAML), developed by the *Security Services Technical Committee of OASIS*, is an XML-based framework for communicating user authentication, entitlement and attribute information. SAML allows business entities to make assertions regarding the identity, attributes, and entitlements of a subject (an entity that is often a human user) to other entities, such as a partner company or another enterprise.

The module `application.SAML` is also:

- A set of XML-based protocol messages
- A set of protocol message bindings
- A set of profiles (utilizing all of the above)

Identity Provider (**IdP**) is a system that creates, maintains, and manages identity information for principals (users, services, or systems), and provides principal authentication to other service providers (applications) within a federation or distributed network.

Service Provider (**SP**) is any system that provides services, typically the services for which users seek authentication, including web or enterprise applications. A special type of service provider, the identity provider, administers identity information.

For more information on SAML, IdP, and SP, you can also refer to the following links:

```
http://xml.coverpages.org/saml.html
http://kb.mit.edu/confluence/display/glossary/
IdP+(Identity+Provider)
https://searchsecurity.techtarget.com/definition/SAML
```

Spring Security has a top-level project named Spring Security SAML. It is considered an extension providing Spring applications to integrate with a variety of authentication and federation mechanisms that supports SAML 2.0. This extension also supports multiple SAML 2.0, profiles as well as IdP and SP initiated SSO.

There are a number of SAML 2.0 compliant products (IdP mode), such as **Okta**, **Ping Federate**, and **ADFS**, that can be integrated into your application quite easily using this Spring Security extension.

Going into detail on SAML is out of the scope of this book. However, we will try to integrate a Spring Boot application that we built earlier, in `Chapter 2`, *Deep Diving into Spring Security*, to tweak and convert it into authentication with an SAML 2.0 product: Okta. In the world of SSO, Okta is a well-known product, allowing applications to easily achieve SSO. In the following example, we will also be using the `spring-security-saml-dsl` project, a Spring Security extension project containing Okta DSL. The use of this eases Spring Security and Okta integration quite significantly. We will also run you through configurations that you will have to use in the Okta platform, to make sure that the example is self-contained and complete. This does not mean that you have to use Okta as the SSO platform for your application; instead, it showcases the Spring Security SAML module, using Okta as an example.

As mentioned previously, we will copy the Spring Boot project that we created in Chapter 2, *Deep Diving into Spring Security*, as a head start for this example. Now, let's go ahead and look at how we can set up the SSO provider (Okta) first; in subsequent sections, we will look at how we can tweak our copied Spring Boot application to achieve SAML 2.0 authentication.

Setting up an SSO provider

As detailed, we will be using Okta as our SSO provider to build our sample application, which covers Spring Security using SAML 2.0 as the authentication mechanism.

To set up an Okta user, perform the following steps:

1. Go to `https://developer.okta.com` and click on **SIGN UP**.
2. Enter the relevant details and click on **GET STARTED**.
3. Okta will send you an email with your **Org Subdomain** and **Temporary Password**.
4. Click on the **Sign In** button in the email, enter your **Username** (email) and **Temporary Password**, and log in.
5. You will be presented with some more account-related information. Fill in the details and complete your account setup.
6. You now have an Okta account set up with one user (you) and no applications configured to do SSO.

Authentication Using SAML, LDAP, and OAuth/OIDC

To set up the Okta application, perform the following steps:

1. Log in to your account and click on the **Admin** button.
2. On the screen, click on the **Add Applications** shortcut link.
3. Click on the **Create New App** button. Select **Web** as the platform, select the **SAML 2.0** radio button, and click on the **Create** button.
4. In the **App name** field, enter your app name, keep the rest of the fields as they are, and click on the **Next** button.
5. In the **Single sign on URL** field, enter the URL as `https://localhost:8443/saml/SSO`. In the **Audience URI** field, enter the URI as `https://localhost:8443/saml/metadata`. Keep the rest of the fields as they are, and click on the **Next** button.
6. Click on the radio button that says **I'm an Okta customer adding an internal app**.
7. Select the checkbox that says, **This is an internal app that we have created**, and click on the **Finish** button.

To assign an Okta application to a user, you need to follow the following steps:

1. Navigate to the dashboard and click on the **Assign Applications** shortcut link.
2. Click on the created application (in the **Applications** section) on the left, click on your username (on the **People** section) on the right, and click on the **Next** button.
3. On the next page, click on the **Confirm Assignments** button, and you will be done assigning the application to a user.

You have now created the Okta application, and your user assignment is complete. Now, let's try modifying the application created earlier, so as to authenticate users using SAML 2.0, against the Okta application we created.

Setting up the project

We will be changing two files: namely, `SpringSecuirtyConfig` (the Spring Security configuration file) and the Spring application properties file (`application.yml`). In the earlier application, instead of a YML (YAML) file, we used a properties file (`application.properties`). In this example, we will discard the `application.properties` file and will use the `application.yml` file for all of the setup. Let's begin now.

[76]

The pom.xml file setup

Copy your previous project. Open the `pom.xml` file and add the following dependencies:

```xml
<!-- SAML2 -->
<dependency>
    <groupId>org.springframework.security.extensions</groupId>
    <artifactId>spring-security-saml2-core</artifactId>
    <version>1.0.3.RELEASE</version>
</dependency>
<dependency>
    <groupId>org.springframework.security.extensions</groupId>
    <artifactId>spring-security-saml-dsl-core</artifactId>
    <version>1.0.5.RELEASE</version>
</dependency>
```

The application.yml file setup

Create a new `application.yml` file in the `src/main/resources` folder with the following content:

```yaml
server:
 port: 8443
 ssl:
   enabled: true
   key-alias: spring
   key-store: src/main/resources/saml/keystore.jks
   key-store-password: secret

security:
 saml2:
   metadata-url:
https://dev-858930.oktapreview.com/app/exkequgfgcSQUrK1N0h7/sso/saml/metadata

spring:
 mvc:
   view:
     prefix: /WEB-INF/views/
     suffix: .jsp
```

In lines 13-17 (in the `spring` section), we have migrated the configuration data that we had in the `application.properties` file into a YML format. You can keep all the preceding configuration same apart from the configurations of `metadata-url` file. For this, you have to go back to the Okta application that you created and navigate to the **Sign On** tab. Now, click on the **Identity Provider** metadata link and copy the link. It will look similar to the one shown previously, with `metadata` at the end of the URL.

The Spring Security configuration files

Now, we will change (or rather, configure) our Spring Security configuration files, as follows:

```
@EnableWebSecurity
@Configuration
@EnableGlobalMethodSecurity(securedEnabled = true)
public class SpringSecurityConfig extends WebSecurityConfigurerAdapter {

    @Value("${security.saml2.metadata-url}")
    String metadataUrl;

    @Override
    protected void configure(HttpSecurity http) throws Exception {
        http
                .authorizeRequests()
                .antMatchers("/saml/**").permitAll()
                .anyRequest().authenticated()
                .and()
                .apply(saml())
                .serviceProvider()
                .keyStore()
                .storeFilePath("saml/keystore.jks")
                .password("secret")
                .keyname("spring")
                .keyPassword("secret")
                .and()
                .protocol("https")
                .hostname("localhost:8443")
                .basePath("/")
                .and()
                .identityProvider()
                .metadataFilePath(metadataUrl)
                .and();
    }
}
```

The file does not have to be modified in any way. It's good to go, through the all-important `configure` method. In `spring-security-saml-dsl-core`, the introduction of the `saml()` method makes coding very concise and easy. With this, you are almost done, and the final step is to create the keystore.

The resources folder setup

Navigate to your project (in the `src/main/resources` folder). Create a folder named `saml` and open the Command Prompt in that location. Execute the following command:

```
keytool -genkey -v -keystore keystore.jks -alias spring -keyalg RSA -
keysize 2048 -validity 10000
```

When prompted, give the required details and create the `keystore.jks` file within the `src/main/resources/saml` folder.

Running and testing the application

Navigate to your project folder and execute the `spring-boot` command, as follows:

```
mvn spring-boot:run
```

Open a browser and navigate to `https://localhost:8443`. Please note the `https` and the port `8443` (because we have SSL enabled). If you don't put `https` in your URL, you will get the following response:

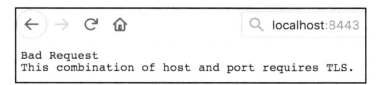

Figure 1: Browser response when HTTP is used

The browser will show a page stating that **Your connection is not secure**. The message may vary, depending on the browser that you choose to open this URL. Just make sure that you accept the risks and move forward.

You will be navigated to the Okta URL, asking you to log in using your username/password, as shown in the following screenshot:

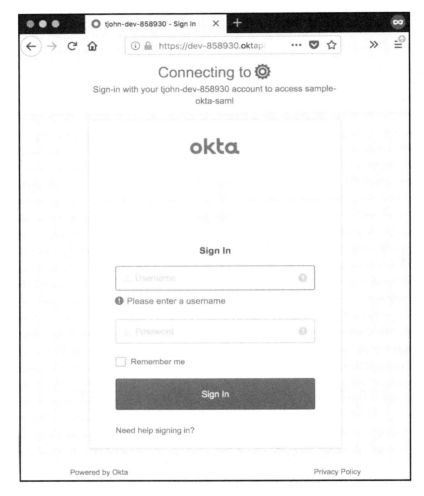

Figure 2: Okta login page shown to the user

Once it's done, you will be navigated back to the home page, showing what you have put in your home.jsp file. The next time you open the URL, you will be taken directly to the home page, and Okta will automatically sign you in.

This completes SAML authentication using Spring Security. You can see the full project by accessing the GitHub page and navigating to the spring-boot-in-memory-saml2-authentication project.

Lightweight Directory Access Protocol

Lightweight Directory Access Protocol (LDAP) is a directory service protocol that allows for connecting, searching, and modifying internet directories. Unfortunately, LDAP doesn't support reactive bindings; this means that reactive programming is not possible (similar to JDBC) with it. The function of LDAP authentication is shown in the following diagram:

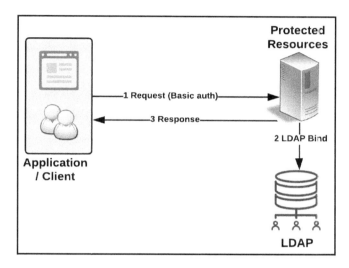

Figure 3: LDAP authentication

Similar to the previous example, we will clone/copy the previous project (any Spring Boot project will do; I am cloning the `spring-boot-in-memory-saml2-authentication` project). Again, similar to the previous project, we will modify a couple of files and add a few more files to the project. We will use the built-in Java-based LDAP server to validate the user credentials.

Set up dependencies in the pom.xml file

Open `pom.xml` and add the following dependencies:

```
<!-- LDAP -->
<dependency>
    <groupId>org.springframework</groupId>
    <artifactId>spring-tx</artifactId>
</dependency>
<dependency>
```

```
      <groupId>org.springframework.ldap</groupId>
      <artifactId>spring-ldap-core</artifactId>
</dependency>
<dependency>
      <groupId>org.springframework.security</groupId>
      <artifactId>spring-security-ldap</artifactId>
</dependency>
<dependency>
      <groupId>com.unboundid</groupId>
      <artifactId>unboundid-ldapsdk</artifactId>
</dependency>
```

Spring Security configuration

Modify the `SpringSecurityConfiguration.java` file, as follows:

```
@EnableWebSecurity
@Configuration
@EnableGlobalMethodSecurity(securedEnabled = true)
public class SpringSecurityConfig extends WebSecurityConfigurerAdapter {
    private static final Logger LOG =
                  LoggerFactory.getLogger(SpringSecurityConfig.class);
    @Override
    protected void configure(HttpSecurity http) throws Exception {
        http.authorizeRequests()
.antMatchers("/admins").hasRole("ADMINS")
                .antMatchers("/users").hasRole("USERS")
                .anyRequest().fullyAuthenticated()
                .and()
                .httpBasic(); // Use Basic authentication
    }
    @Override
    public void configure(AuthenticationManagerBuilder auth) throws
Exception {
        auth
                .ldapAuthentication()
                .userDnPatterns("uid={0},ou=people")
                .userSearchBase("ou=people")
                .userSearchFilter("uid={0}")
                .groupSearchBase("ou=groups")
                .groupSearchFilter("uniqueMember={0}")
                .contextSource(contextSource())
                .passwordCompare()
                .passwordAttribute("userPassword");
    }
    @Bean
```

```
public DefaultSpringSecurityContextSource contextSource() {
    LOG.info("Inside configuring embedded LDAP server");
    DefaultSpringSecurityContextSource contextSource = new
            DefaultSpringSecurityContextSource(
            Arrays.asList("ldap://localhost:8389/"),
"dc=packtpub,dc=com");
    contextSource.afterPropertiesSet();
    return contextSource;
}
}
```

The first `configure` method is very similar to what we saw in the previous SAML example. We have just added certain matches and separated the roles. With these changes, it will still perform basic authentication.

The second `configure` method is where we have set up authentication using the LDAP server. The LDAP server stores user information in a directory-like format. This method details how to find the user by navigating through the directory structure.

LDAP server setup

We are going to use Spring's default LDAP server to store our users, and then use this as a user store against which we can authenticate the users in our application. The LDAP configuration is done in our `application.yml` file, as follows:

```
spring:
 ldap:
   # Embedded Spring LDAP
   embedded:
     base-dn: dc=packtpub,dc=com
     credential:
       username: uid=admin
       password: secret
     ldif: classpath:ldap/ldapschema.ldif
     port: 8389
     validation:
       enabled: false
 mvc:
   view:
     prefix: /WEB-INF/views/
     suffix: .jsp
```

The `ldap` section is self-explanatory—we are setting up the embedded LDAP server with various parameters.

Setting up users in the LDAP server

We are going to use the **LDAP Data Interchange Format** (**LDIF**) to set up our users on our LDAP server. The LDIF is a standard text-based representation for LDAP data, and changes to that data (https://ldap.com/ldif-the-ldap-data-interchange-format/).

In our application.yml file, we have shown Spring where to look for our LDIF file. The LDIF file is as follows:

```
dn: dc=packtpub,dc=com
objectclass: top
objectclass: domain
objectclass: extensibleObject
dc: packtpub

dn: ou=groups,dc=packtpub,dc=com
objectclass: top
objectclass: organizationalUnit
ou: groups

dn: ou=people,dc=packtpub,dc=com
objectclass: top
objectclass: organizationalUnit
ou: people

dn: uid=john,ou=people,dc=packtpub,dc=com
objectclass: top
objectclass: person
objectclass: organizationalPerson
objectclass: inetOrgPerson
cn: Tomcy John
uid: tjohn
userPassword: tjohn@password

dn: cn=admins,ou=groups,dc=packtpub,dc=com
objectclass: top
objectclass: groupOfUniqueNames
cn: admins
ou: admin
uniqueMember: uid=tjohn,ou=people,dc=packtpub,dc=com

dn: cn=users,ou=groups,dc=packtpub,dc=com
objectclass: top
objectclass: groupOfUniqueNames
cn: users
ou: user
uniqueMember: uid=tjohn,ou=people,dc=packtpub,dc=com
```

Running the application

There are not many changes in any of the other files within the project. Just like you run any other `spring-boot` project, go to the project folder and execute the following command:

```
mvn spring-boot:run
```

Seeing the application in action on a browser

Open a browser and enter `http://localhost:8080`. Enter the username/password as `tjohn/tjohn@password` (look for user setup in the LDIF file). You will be taken to `home.jsp`, where you will see a friendly welcome message, as shown in the following screenshot:

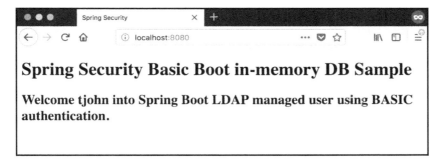

Figure 4: Message shown in home.jsp page after successful login using LDAP

OAuth2 and OpenID Connect

OAuth is an open standard/specification for achieving authorization. It works over HTTPS, and anyone can implement the specification. The specification works by validating access tokens, and then authorizes devices, APIs, servers, and so on.

Two versions—namely OAuth 1.0 (`https://tools.ietf.org/html/rfc5849`) and OAuth 2.0 (`https://tools.ietf.org/html/rfc6749`)—exist. These versions are not compatible with each other and cannot work together. We will use version 2.0 and it will be referred to as OAuth 2.0, throughout this book.

SAML, released in 2005, is a good fit for the web browser (still). But with modern web and native applications (mobile devices), SAML required a serious overhaul, and that's when OAuth came in. **Single Page Applications** (**SPAs**) and native applications are different from traditional server-side web applications. SPAs do AJAX/XHR calls to the APIs that are exposed on the server and does many other operations on the client (browser). API development has also changed, from heavy SOAP-based web services using XML to lightweight REST over HTTP using JSON.

OAuth also enables you, as a developer, to gain access to minimal user data without having to give away a user's password. It is mainly for accessing the APIs (REST) exposed by an application, and is done by delegating the authorization function.

OAuth supports a variety of application types and decouples authentication from authorization.

In simple terms, this is how OAuth works:

1. The app that wants to access resources requests the user to grant authorization.
2. If the user authorizes it, the app is given proof for this agreement.
3. Using this proof, the app goes to the actual server with the APIs and gets a token.
4. Using this token, the app can now ask for resources (APIs) to which the user has given access, while giving the proof.

The preceding steps are depicted in the following diagram:

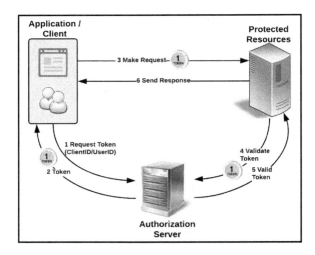

Figure 5: Functionality of OAuth

OAuth was tweaked in such a way by using an access token, apps can get user information in the form of an API. Facebook Connect (an SSO application that allows users to interact with other web applications using Facebook credentials) used this as a mechanism to expose an endpoint (http(s)://<domain>/me) that would return minimal user information. This was never clearly there in OAuth specification, and this provoked **Open ID Connect (OIDC)**, which combined the best parts of OAuth2, Facebook Connect, and SAML 2.0. OIDC brought in a new ID token (id_token), and also a UserInfo endpoint that will provide minimal user attributes. Many of the complexities that SAML had, and many of the shortcomings of OAuth2 were addressed by OIDC.

Going deep, into OAuth and OIDC is not in the scope of this book. I am sure that I have given adequate information, using which you can navigate through the rest of this section.

Setting up a project

The example code that we are going to create here has a different approach from our earlier samples. Here, we will use *Spring Initializr* (http://start.spring.io/) to create the base project, and then we will inject the appropriate changes to make it log in with a provider, namely, Google.

Bootstrap Spring project using Spring Initializr

Visit http://start.spring.io/ and enter the following details. Make sure that you select the right dependencies:

Figure 6: Spring Initializr setup

Click on the **Generate Project** button and download the ZIP file to a folder of your choice. Execute the `unzip` command as follows. I am using Macintosh for running all of my sample applications, so I will be using commands, if any, suitable for this platform:

```
unzip -a spring-boot-oauth-oidc-authentication.zip
```

Inclusion of OAuth libraries in pom.xml

Modify your project's `pom.xml` file by adding the following dependencies:

```xml
<!-- Provided -->
<dependency>
  <groupId>org.springframework.boot</groupId>
  <artifactId>spring-boot-starter-tomcat</artifactId>
  <scope>provided</scope>
</dependency>
<dependency>
  <groupId>org.apache.tomcat.embed</groupId>
  <artifactId>tomcat-embed-jasper</artifactId>
  <scope>provided</scope>
</dependency>
<!-- OAuth -->
<dependency>
  <groupId>org.springframework.boot</groupId>
  <artifactId>spring-boot-starter-security</artifactId>
</dependency>
<dependency>
  <groupId>org.springframework.security</groupId>
  <artifactId>spring-security-oauth2-client</artifactId>
</dependency>
<dependency>
  <groupId>org.springframework.security</groupId>
  <artifactId>spring-security-oauth2-jose</artifactId>
</dependency>
```

Setting up provider details in application.properties

If you run the application (`./mvnw spring-boot:run`) and then navigate your browser to `http://localhost:8080`, you will see a default login page, as follows. The entire magic behind this page is done for you by Spring Boot and Spring Security:

Figure 7: Default Spring Boot + Spring Security project created using Spring Initializr

Open the `application.properties` file (`src/main/resources`) and add the following properties:

```
#Google app details
spring.security.oauth2.client.registration.google.client-id=1085570125650-
18j2r88b5i5gbe3vkhtlf8j7u3hvdu78.apps.googleusercontent.com
spring.security.oauth2.client.registration.google.client-secret=MdzcKp-
ArG51FeqfAUw4K8Mp
#Facebook app details
spring.security.oauth2.client.registration.facebook.client-
id=229630157771581
spring.security.oauth2.client.registration.facebook.client-
secret=e37501e8adfc160d6c6c9e3c8cc5fc0b
#Github app details
spring.security.oauth2.client.registration.github.client-id=<your client
id>
spring.security.oauth2.client.registration.github.client-secret=<your
client secret>
#Spring MVC details
spring.mvc.view.prefix: /WEB-INF/views/
spring.mvc.view.suffix: .jsp
```

Here, we declare two properties for each provider. We will be implementing the Google provider, but you can add any number of providers. Just adding these properties will create more magic, and your login page will suddenly change to the following:

Figure 8: OAuth default login page when application.properties file is modified

The providers (links) shown in the preceding screenshot are according to the configurations seen in the `application.properties` file. It just looks for two properties, as follows:

```
spring.security.oauth2.client.registration.<provider_name>.client-
id=<client id>
spring.security.oauth2.client.registration.<provider_name>.client-
secret=<client secret>
```

Provider setup

We will be using Google as our provider in this example. Navigate to `https://console.developers.google.com/` and perform the following steps:

1. Create a project. Select an existing project or create a new project, as shown in the following screenshot:

Figure 9: Project creation

2. Create the credentials. Select the newly created project (in the following screenshot, it is shown next to the **Google APIs** logo) and click on the **Credentials** link in the side menu, as shown in the following screenshot:

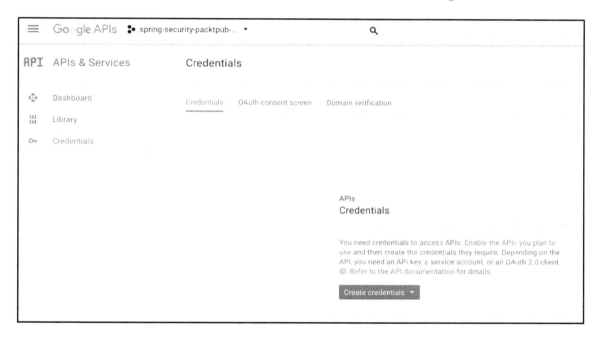

Figure 10: Credential creation - step 1

3. Now, click on the **Create credentials** drop-down menu, as shown in the following screenshot:

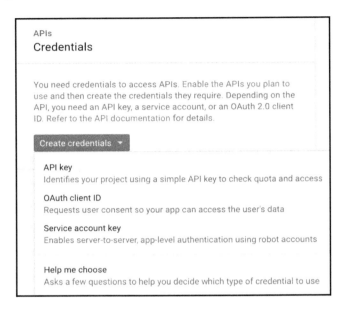

Figure 11: Credential creation - step 2

4. From the drop-down menu, click on **OAuth client ID**. This will navigate you to the page shown in the following screenshot. Please note that the **Application type** radio group will be disabled at this stage:

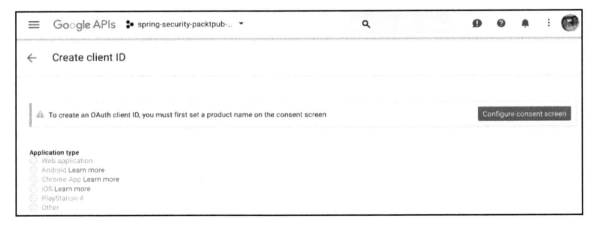

Figure 12: Credential creation - step 3

5. Click on **Configure consent screen**. You will be navigated to the following page:

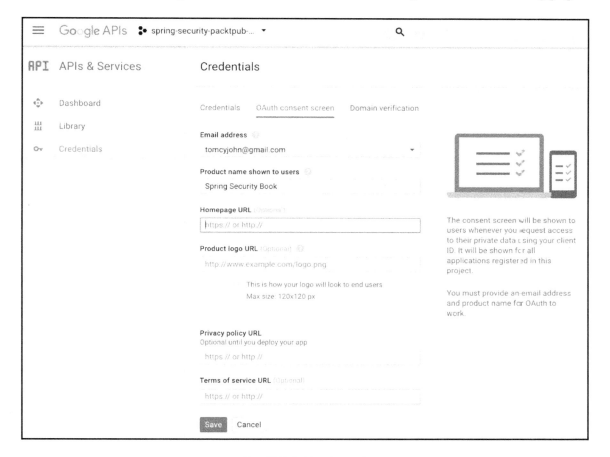

Figure 13: Credential creation - step 4

6. Enter the relevant details (leave the optional fields out while filling in the form), as shown in the preceding figure, and click on the **Save** button. You will be navigated back to the page shown in the following figure.

This time, the **Application type** radio group will be enabled:

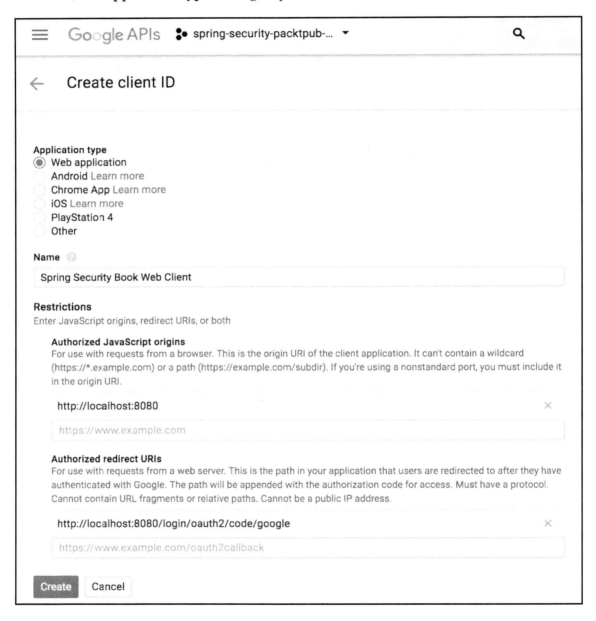

7. Select the **Application type** as **Web application**, and enter the relevant details, as shown in the preceding figure. Click on the **Create** button, and you will be shown the following popup:

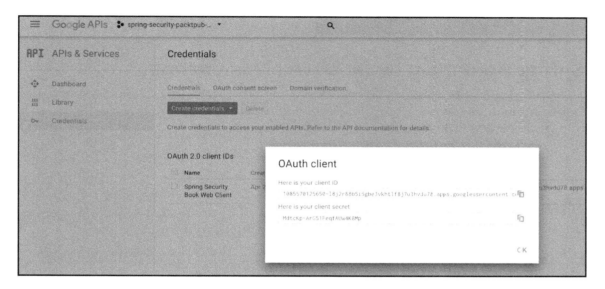

Figure 15: Credential creation - step 6

You now have your client ID and client secret from Google. Copy and paste these values into the `application.properties` file in the correct place.

Default application change

To be in line with the previous example, we will make changes in the default application that was generated, bringing in the same components seen in the previous application. This will help you to understand the application in detail.

The HomeController class

Copy the home controller class (`HomeController.java`) that we created in our previous example to a new package. Change the welcome message to whatever you want.

The home.jsp file

Copy the whole `webapp` folder from the previous example, as is, into this project. Change the page heading to something different so that it is clear while running the application that it is indeed the sample application.

Spring Boot main application class change

Make your application class extend the `SpringBootServletInitializer` class. Add a new annotation, as follows, letting your Spring Boot application know that a new controller, `HomeController`, is a component that it has to scan:

```
@ComponentScan(basePackageClasses=HomeController.class)
```

Running the application

Run your application by executing the following default command:

```
./mvnw spring-boot:run
```

If all is well, you should be able to click on the Google link, and it should navigate you to the Google's login page. After successfully logging in, you will be redirected to the `home.jsp` file, as shown in the following screenshot:

Figure 16: Login using Google as OAuth provider

The support for OAuth doesn't end here, but we have to stop, as the book cannot delve deeply into the many aspects that the framework provides.

Summary

In this chapter, we saw authentication mechanisms commonly used in the enterprises, namely SAML, LDAP, and OAuth/OIDC, supported by Spring Security through hands-on coding examples. We used the sample application built as part of `Chapter 2`, *Deep Diving into Spring Security*, as a basis for explaining the functionality and implementation of other authentication mechanisms.

However, we intentionally didn't reactive programming in our coding examples. This chapter was aimed at making you understand the core concepts of each of the authentication mechanisms, by making use of the familiar Spring Web MVC application framework. We will cover reactive programming in more detail in `Chapter 5`, *Integrating with Spring WebFlux*.

Authentication Using CAS and JAAS

This chapter picks up from where we left off in the previous chapter by looking at other authentication mechanisms, namely CAS and JAAS, supported by Spring Security. Again, this is also a fully hands-on coding chapter, and we will build small applications, most of them starting from the base application that we built in Chapter 2, *Deep Diving into Spring Security*. These authentication mechanisms are well-known in the industry and many enterprises have these as established mechanism by which they authenticate the user and give access to many of their employee and consumer facing applications.

Each of the authentication mechanisms has a project that you can see in the book's GitHub page. However, in the book, we will only cover important aspects of the sample code to reduce clutter within the chapter.

In this chapter, we will cover the following topics:

- CAS
- Java Authentication and Authorization Service
- Kerberos
- Custom AuthenticationEntryPoint
- Password Encoder
- Custom Filter

CAS

The Central Authentication Service (CAS) is a single-sign-on/single-sign-off protocol for the web. It permits a user to access multiple applications while providing their credentials (such as userid and password) only once to a central CAS Server application.

– CAS Protocol Specification

CAS is an open source, platform-independent, central **single sign-on** (**SSO**) service supporting a variety of well-known protocols. Spring Security has first-class support for CAS, and the implementation is quite simple for an enterprise having a central CAS server. CAS is based on Spring Framework, and the architecture is quite simple, as shown in the following diagram:

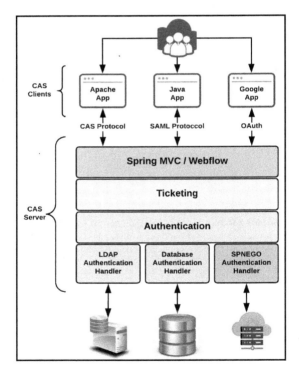

Figure 1: CAS architecture (figure adapted from https://apereo.github.io)

The **CAS server** is a Java servlet-based application built on Spring Framework (Spring MVC and Spring Web Flow). It authenticates and grants access to CAS-enabled services.

Upon the successful login of the user, an SSO session is created, and the server issues a **ticket-granting-ticket** (**TGT**), and this token is validated against the backend for subsequent calls from the client.

The **CAS client** is a CAS-enabled application that communicates with CAS using supported protocols (CAS, SAML, OAuth, and so on). A number of language supports are a ready available for CAS, and a number of applications have implemented this methodology. Some of the well-known applications are Atlassian products (JIRA and Confluence), Drupal, and so on.

The following diagram shows the authentication flow (sequence diagram) involving a CAS server and client:

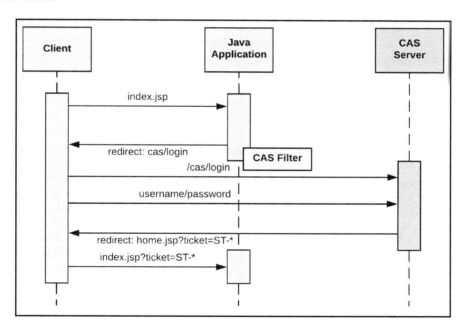

Figure 2: CAS authentication flow

Let's see a working hands-on example now. We will have to create a CAS server and then a client that uses the CAS server to connect and get itself authenticated.

CAS server setup

The CAS project source code can be found in GitHub at `https://github.com/apereo/cas`. It is not really required to check out the source code, build the CAS server, and then deploy it. WAR overlay is an approach wherein, rather than downloading the source and building, we get a pre-built CAS web application and then we can customize certain behavior as needed for achieving our use case. We will be using this approach to set up our CAS server. Also, we will use Maven-based WAR overlay, which can be found in GitHub at `https://github.com/apereo/cas-overlay-template`.

Git clone

Launch your favorite command prompt and clone the CAS overlay project into your desired project. I am going to create a folder named `cas-sample`, wherein I will clone the server in the `server` folder by executing the following command from the `cas-sample` folder:

```
git clone https://github.com/apereo/cas-overlay-template.git server
```

Adding additional dependencies

The CAS server doesn't allow any client to connect to it. Each client has to be registered with the desired CAS server. There are multiple mechanisms by which we can register a client to the server. We will use the JSON/YML configuration to register our client to the server. Go ahead and add the following dependency to your `pom.xml` file within the server project that you just cloned:

```
<dependency>
    <groupId>org.apereo.cas</groupId>
    <artifactId>cas-server-support-json-service-registry</artifactId>
    <version>${cas.version}</version>
</dependency>
<dependency>
    <groupId>org.apereo.cas</groupId>
    <artifactId>cas-server-support-yaml-service-registry</artifactId>
    <version>${cas.version}</version>
</dependency>
```

Most of the versions in the `pom.xml` file are managed by the parent POM.

Setting up the resources folder in the project

In the `server` project, create a folder called `src/main/resources`. Copy the `etc` folder within the `server` folder into `src/main/resources`:

```
mkdir -p src/main/resources
cp -R etc src/main/resources
```

Creating the application.properties file

Create a file named `application.properties`:

```
touch src/main/resources/application.properties
```

Now fill in the following details in the `application.properties` file:

```
server.context-path=/cas
server.port=6443

server.ssl.key-store=classpath:/etc/cas/thekeystore
server.ssl.key-store-password=changeit
server.ssl.key-password=changeit

cas.server.name: https://localhost:6443
cas.server.prefix: https://localhost:6443/cas

cas.adminPagesSecurity.ip=127\.0\.0\.1

cas.authn.accept.users=casuser::password
```

The preceding file sets the port and SSL keystore values (a very important step in setting up a CAS server), and also sets up the CAS server `config` folder. Clearly, we need to create a keystore as indicated in this file.

Please note, the overlay project has a file, namely the `build.sh` file, that contains most of these details in it. We are manually doing this to have a clear understanding.

The last line in `application.properties` sets up a test user with the credentials `casuser`/`password`, which can be used to log into the CAS server for various demo purposes. This approach is not recommended in the production setup.

Creating a local SSL keystore

Navigate to the `cas-sample/server/src/main/resources/etc/cas` folder in a shell and execute the following command:

```
keytool -genkey -keyalg RSA -alias thekeystore -keystore thekeystore -
storepass password -validity 360 -keysize 2048
```

The following figure shows the successful execution of the preceding command in a command prompt window:

```
➜  cas git:(master) ✗ keytool -genkey -keyalg RSA -alias thekeystore -keystore thekeystore -storepass password -validity 360 -keysize 2048
What is your first and last name?
  [Unknown]:  localhost
What is the name of your organizational unit?
  [Unknown]:  localhost
What is the name of your organization?
  [Unknown]:  localhost
What is the name of your City or Locality?
  [Unknown]:  Dubai
What is the name of your State or Province?
  [Unknown]:  Dubai
What is the two-letter country code for this unit?
  [Unknown]:  AE
Is CN=localhost, OU=localhost, O=localhost, L=Dubai, ST=Dubai, C=AE correct?
  [no]:  yes

Enter key password for <thekeystore>
        (RETURN if same as keystore password):
➜  cas git:(master) ✗ ▊
```

Figure 3: Creation of SSL keystore

It's important to note that for the SSL handshake to work properly, most of the values while generating the keystore are put as localhost. This is an important step and needs to be followed without fail.

Creating the .crt file to be used by the client

For the client to connect to the CAS server, out of the generated keystore, we need to create a `.crt` file. In the same folder (`cas-sample/server/src/main/resources/etc/cas`), run the following command:

```
keytool -export -alias thekeystore -file thekeystore.crt -keystore
thekeystore
```

When asked for a password, provide the same password (we have set the password as `password`). Executing the preceding command will create `thekeystore.crt` file.

Exporting the .crt file to Java and the JRE cacert keystore

Execute the following command to find your Java installation directory:

```
/usr/libexec/java_home
```

Alternatively, execute the following command directly to add the `.crt` file to Java cacerts:

```
keytool -import -alias thekeystore -storepass password -file
thekeystore.crt -keystore
"$(/usr/libexec/java_home)\jre\lib\security\cacerts"
```

The following figure shows successful execution of the preceding command in a command prompt window:

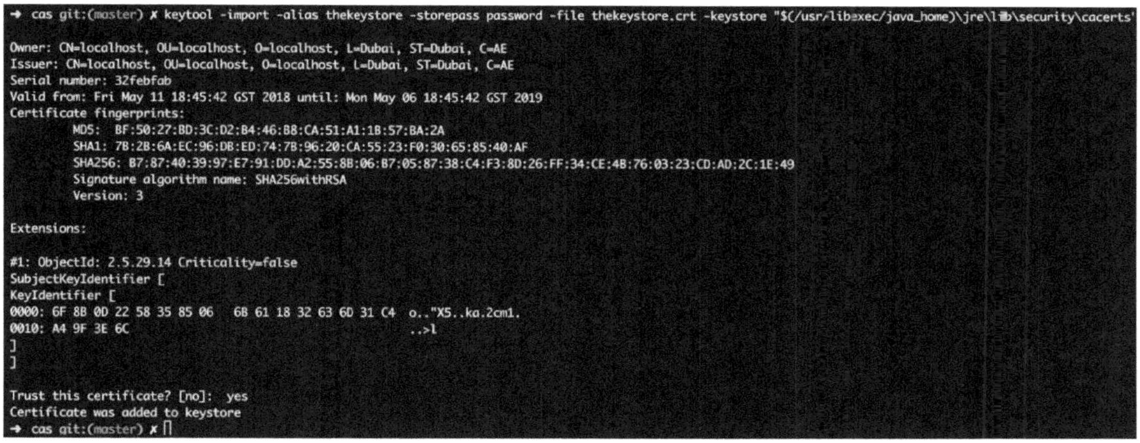

Figure 4: Exporting .crt file to Java keystore

When setting up a client, make sure that the JDK used is the same as the one in which we have added the `.crt` file. To reflect the certification addition on to Java, a restart of the machine is suggested.

Building a CAS server project and running it

From within the cas-sample/cas-server folder, execute the following two commands:

```
./build.sh package
./build.sh run
```

If everything goes well, as shown in the following figure, you should see a log message which says **READY**:

Figure 5: CAS server ready logging

Now open a browser and navigate to the URL `https://localhost:6443/cas`. This will navigate you to the default login form of the CAS server. Enter the default credentials (`casuser/Mellon`) and you are in. Most browsers would say that the connection is insecure. Add the domain as an exception and soon after that the application will work fine:

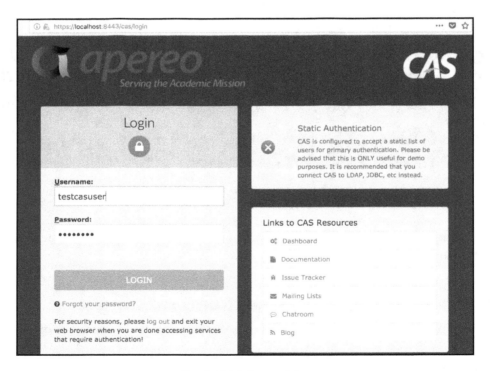

Figure 6: Default CAS server login form

Log in with the demo test user (`testcasuser/password`) and you should be logged in and navigated to a user home page.

Registering a client with the CAS server

As mentioned earlier, every client has to be registered with the CAS server to allow participation in SSO. The section shows how we can register a client with the CAS server.

JSON service configuration

There are many ways by which a client/service can register itself to a CAS server. We will be using JSON configuration here and have already included dependencies to our `pom.xml` file in the earlier step. Apart from JSON, other formats such as YAML, Mongo, LDAP and others do exist.

Create a new folder named `clients` in the `src/main/resources` folder. Create a new file in the newly created folder with the following content:

```
--- !<org.apereo.cas.services.RegexRegisteredService>
serviceId: "^(http?|https?)://.*"
name: "YAML"
id: 5000
description: "description"
attributeReleasePolicy:
!<org.apereo.cas.services.ReturnAllAttributeReleasePolicy> {}
accessStrategy:
!<org.apereo.cas.services.DefaultRegisteredServiceAccessStrategy>
 enabled: true
 ssoEnabled: true
```

Save the file with the name `newYmlFile-5000.yml`. Let's go into the details of a couple of important attributes:

- `serviceId`: URL, in a regular expression pattern, of clients who want to connect to the CAS server. In our example, we refer to a client Spring Boot application running on port `9090`, which connects to the CAS server.
- `id`: unique identifier for this configuration.

Other configurable attributes are documented in the official website at `https://goo.gl/CGsDp1`.

Additional application.properties file changes

In this step, we let the CAS server about the usage of YML configuration and the location to find these YMLs in the server. Add the following property to the `application.properties` file:

```
cas.serviceRegistry.yaml.location=classpath:/clients
```

It's good practice to separate CAS-related configuration properties into a different properties file. So, go ahead and create a `cas.properties` file and include CAS-related properties there.

CAS client setup

We will use Spring Initializr to create our CAS client project setup. We used a similar approach earlier. Let's go through it once again.

Bootstrap Spring project using Spring Initializr

Visit `http://start.spring.io/` and enter the following details as shown in the following figure. Make sure you select the right dependencies:

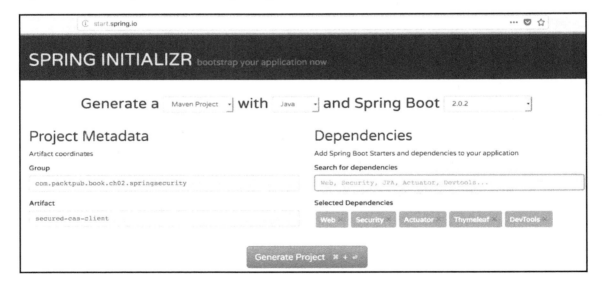

Figure 7: Spring Initializr for creating secured-cas-client project

Click on the **Generate Project** button and download the ZIP file to a folder of your choice (I will be keeping this inside the `cas-sample` folder). Execute the `unzip` command as follows. I am using macOS for running all my sample application, so I will be using commands, if any, suitable for this platform:

```
unzip -a spring-boot-cas-client.zip
```

Including CAS libraries in pom.xml

Modify your project's `pom.xml` by adding the following dependencies:

```
<dependency>
    <groupId>org.springframework.security</groupId>
    <artifactId>spring-security-cas</artifactId>
</dependency>
```

Changing the application.properties file

Just to make sure that we don't use any other commonly used ports, we are going to set the client to listen to port `9090`. In the CAS server, we have also configured it so that the client will be listening to port `9090`. Add the following property to the `application.properties` file:

```
server.port=9090
```

Additional bean configuration

We will now set up various beans, as needed by the CAS Spring Security module.

ServiceProperties bean

Convey to CAS that this is your CAS client/service by setting up this bean.
Open `SpringBootCasClientApplication.java` and add the following bean definition:

```
@Bean
public ServiceProperties serviceProperties() {
ServiceProperties serviceProperties = new ServiceProperties();
    serviceProperties.setService("http://localhost:9090/login/cas");
    serviceProperties.setSendRenew(false);
    return serviceProperties;
}
```

The URL `http://localhost:9090/login/cas` that is configured will internally get mapped to `CasAuthenticationFilter`. The parameter `sendRenew` is set to `false`. Being set as `false`, this tells the login service that username/password is required to gain access to the service, every time. It also gives the user access to all services/client without having to enter a username/password (if already done once). When logged out, the user is logged out automatically from all services.

AuthenticationEntryPoint bean

Take a look at the following code. Quite straightforward, isn't it?. This is where we let know where our CAS server is running. When a user tries to log in, the application will be redirected to this URL:

```
@Bean
public AuthenticationEntryPoint authenticationEntryPoint() {
    CasAuthenticationEntryPoint casAuthEntryPoint = new
CasAuthenticationEntryPoint();
    casAuthEntryPoint.setLoginUrl("https://localhost:6443/cas/login");
    casAuthEntryPoint.setServiceProperties(serviceProperties());
    return casAuthEntryPoint;
}
```

TicketValidator bean

When the client application gets a ticket that has already been given to a particular user, this bean is used to validate its authenticity:

```
@Bean
public TicketValidator ticketValidator() {
    return new Cas30ServiceTicketValidator("https://localhost:6443/cas");
}
```

CasAuthenticationProvider bean

Bind all the beans declared earlier to the authentication provider bean. We will be loading users from a static list provided as part of `UserDetailsService` in the authentication provider. In a production scenario, this will point to a database:

```
@Bean
public CasAuthenticationProvider casAuthenticationProvider() {
  CasAuthenticationProvider provider = new CasAuthenticationProvider();
  provider.setServiceProperties(serviceProperties());
  provider.setTicketValidator(ticketValidator());
  provider.setUserDetailsService((s) -> new User("casuser", "password",
      true, true, true, true,
```

```
                   AuthorityUtils.createAuthorityList("ROLE_ADMIN")));
        provider.setKey("CAS_PROVIDER_PORT_9090");
        return provider;
    }
```

With this we are ready to set up the all-important Spring Security configuration.

Setting up Spring Security

Let's bring in the bean references that we have done in the previous step to the Spring Security configuration file. Create a new Java file called SpringSecurityConfig and add member variables. After that, create a constructor with @Autowired annotation as follows:

```
    private AuthenticationProvider authenticationProvider;
    private AuthenticationEntryPoint authenticationEntryPoint:

    @Autowired
    public SpringSecurityConfig(CasAuthenticationProvider
    casAuthenticationProvider,
                    AuthenticationEntryPoint authenticationEntryPoint) {
        this.authenticationProvider = casAuthenticationProvider;
        this.authenticationEntryPoint = authenticationEntryPcint;
    }
```

When a user accesses a client application that is secured by a CAS server, the configured bean AuthenticationEntryPoint is triggered, and the user is taken to the CAS server URL that is configured in this bean. Once the user enters credentials and submits the page, the CAS server authenticates the user and creates a service ticket. This ticket is now appended to the URL and the user is taken to the requested client application. The client application uses the TicketValidator bean to validate the ticket with the CAS server and, if valid, allows user to access the requested page.

We need to override a couple of important methods before we configure our HTTP security. The first method uses AuthenticationManagerBuilder, in which we tell it to use our AuthenticationProvider. Please create the method as follows:

```
    @Override
    protected void configure(AuthenticationManagerBuilder auth) throws
    Exception {
        auth.authenticationProvider(authenticationProvider);
    }
```

We now override another method that indicates to the `AuthenticationManager` to put our created `AuthenticationProvider` in it:

```
@Override
protected AuthenticationManager authenticationManager() throws Exception {
    return new ProviderManager(Arrays.asList(authenticationProvider));
}
```

We are now ready to create a filter named `CasAuthenticationFilter` (as a bean), which actually intercepts the requests and does CAS ticket validation.

Creating the CasAuthenticationFilter bean

Creating the `CasAuthenticationFilter` bean is quite straightforward, as we just assign the `serviceProperties` that we created to the `CasAuthenticationFilter`:

```
@Bean
public CasAuthenticationFilter casAuthenticationFilter(ServiceProperties
serviceProperties) throws Exception {
    CasAuthenticationFilter filter = new CasAuthenticationFilter();
    filter.setServiceProperties(serviceProperties);
    filter.setAuthenticationManager(authenticationManager());
    return filter;
}
```

Setting up the controller

This is the final setup in our CAS client project setup. We will have an unsecured page containing a link to a secured page. When the secured page is accessed, CAS SSO kicks in and the user is navigated to the CAS authentication page. Once you log in using the credentials (`casuser`/`password`), the user is taken to the secured page, where we display the authenticated username.

We will create an `ndexController` that has the root folder routing (`/`). This navigates the user to the `index.html` page.

Create `IndexController.java` in a new package (preferably in the controllers package):

```
@Controller
public class IndexController {
    @GetMapping("/")
    public String index() {
        return "index";
    }
}
```

Create the `index.html` file in the `src/resources/templates` folder with the following content:

```
<!DOCTYPE html>
<html xmlns:th="http://www.thymeleaf.org">
<head>
    <meta charset="UTF-8" />
    <title>Spring Security CAS Sample - Unsecured page</title>
</head>
<body>
<h1>Spring Security CAS Sample - Unsecured page</h1>
<br>
<a href="/secured">Go to Secured Page</a>
</body>
</html>
```

Now create a new controller named `CasController.java` within the same controllers package. We will be mapping all secured pages as well as setting up various request mappings in this controller. In the controller class, copy the following code snippet:

```
@Controller
@RequestMapping(value = "/secured")
public class CasController {

    @GetMapping
    public String secured(ModelMap modelMap) {
        Authentication auth =
SecurityContextHolder.getContext().getAuthentication();
        if( auth != null && auth.getPrincipal() != null
            && auth.getPrincipal() instanceof UserDetails) {
          modelMap.put("authusername", ((UserDetails)
auth.getPrincipal()).getUsername());
        }
        return "secured";
    }
}
```

Create a new HTML file named `secured.html` with the following content. This is our secured page and will just display the authenticated username:

```
<!DOCTYPE html>
<html xmlns:th="http://www.thymeleaf.org">
<head>
    <meta charset="UTF-8" />
    <title>Spring Security CAS Sample - Secured page</title>
</head>
<body>
<h1>Spring Security CAS Sample - Secured page</h1>
```

```
<br>
<h3 th:text="${authusername} ? 'Hello authenticated user, ' +
${authusername} + '!' : 'Hello non-logged in user!'">Hello non-logged in
user!</h3>
</body>
</html>
```

Running the application

Start the CAS server (within `cas-server`, run `./build.sh run`). After that, start the spring boot project (`secured-cas-client`) by executing `./mvnw spring-boot:run`. Navigate your browser to `http://localhost:9090`. This will take the user to `index.html`, and when they click on the link (which navigates to the `secured.html` page), the user is taken to the CAS authentication page. To be authenticated, enter the CAS credentials and, with the ticket set as query string, you will then be taken to the secured page. The secured page validates the ticket with the CAS server and then displays the username.

With this, we complete our CAS sample using Spring Security. In the next section, similar to CAS, we will detail usage of JAAS authentication by employing Spring Security.

Java Authentication and Authorization Service

Java Authentication and Authorization Service (JAAS) (`https://docs.oracle.com/javase/6/docs/technotes/guides/security/jaas/JAASRefGuide.html`) implements a Java version of the standard **Pluggable Authentication Module (PAM)** framework. It was introduced as an optional package (extension) to the J2SDK (1.3) and then was integrated into the J2SDK 1.4.

JAAS is a standard library which provides your application with the following:

- A representation of identity (principal) by providing credentials (username/password – subject).
- A login service that will call back your application to gather credentials from user and then returns a subject after successful authentication.
- A mechanism to grant necessary grants (authorization) to a user after successful authentication:

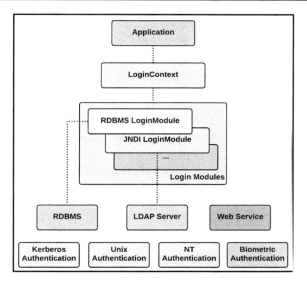

Figure 8: Working of JAAS

As shown in the preceding figure, JAAS has predefined login modules for most of the login mechanisms built in. Custom login modules can be imported or built according to application requirements. JAAS allows application to be independent from the actual authentication mechanism. It's truly pluggable, as new login modules can be integrated without any change to the application code.

JAAS is simple and the process is as follows:

- The application instantiates a `LoginContext` object and invokes appropriate (controlled by configuration) `LoginModule`, which performs authentication.
- Once the authentication is successful, the *subject* (who runs the code) is updated with principle and credentials by `LoginModule`.
- Soon after that, JAAS kick starts the authorization process (using standard Java SE access control model). Access is granted based on the following:
  - **Codesource**: where the code originated and who signed the code
  - **The user**: who (also called as **subject**) is running the code

Now that we have a rough idea of JAAS and its working, we will see working of JAAS using Spring Security by going through an example in the following section.

Setting up a project

The sample application that we are going to build is very similar to the one that we created at the start of `Chapter 3`, *Authentication Using SAML, LDAP, and OAuth/OIDC*. Many aspects are similar but differ in a subtle manner. Each step will be explained; however, at times we won't go into details as we have seen some aspects in earlier samples.

Setting up Maven project

We will be creating a Maven project using the IntelliJ IDE. Add the following dependencies and build setup in your `pom.xml` file:

```
<groupId>com.packtpub.book.ch04.springsecurity</groupId>
<artifactId>jetty-jaas-authentication</artifactId>
<version>1.0-SNAPSHOT</version>
<packaging>war</packaging>
<properties>
    <maven.compiler.source>1.8</maven.compiler.source>
    <maven.compiler.target>1.8</maven.compiler.target>
    <failOnMissingWebXml>false</failOnMissingWebXml>
</properties>
<dependencies>
    <!--Spring Security Dependencies-->
    <dependency>
        <groupId>org.springframework.security</groupId>
        <artifactId>spring-security-web</artifactId>
        <version>5.0.4.RELEASE</version>
    </dependency>
    <dependency>
        <groupId>org.springframework.security</groupId>
        <artifactId>spring-security-config</artifactId>
        <version>5.0.4.RELEASE</version>
    </dependency>
    <!--Spring Framework Dependencies-->
    <dependency>
        <groupId>org.springframework</groupId>
        <artifactId>spring-context</artifactId>
        <version>5.0.4.RELEASE</version>
    </dependency>
    <dependency>
        <groupId>org.springframework</groupId>
```

```
    <artifactId>spring-webmvc</artifactId>
    <version>5.0.4.RELEASE</version>
</dependency>
<!-- JSP, JSTL and Tag Libraries-->
<dependency>
    <groupId>javax.servlet</groupId>
    <artifactId>javax.servlet-api</artifactId>
    <version>3.1.0</version>
    <scope>provided</scope>
</dependency>
<dependency>
    <groupId>javax.servlet</groupId>
    <artifactId>jstl</artifactId>
    <version>1.2</version>
    <scope>provided</scope>
</dependency>
<dependency>
    <groupId>javax.servlet.jsp</groupId>
    <artifactId>javax.servlet.jsp-api</artifactId>
    <version>2.3.1</version>
    <scope>provided</scope>
</dependency>
<dependency>
    <groupId>javax.servlet.jsp.jstl</groupId>
    <artifactId>javax.servlet.jsp.jstl-api</artifactId>
    <version>1.2.1</version>
</dependency>
<dependency>
    <groupId>taglibs</groupId>
    <artifactId>standard</artifactId>
    <version>1.1.2</version>
</dependency>
<!--SLF4J and logback-->
<dependency>
    <groupId>org.slf4j</groupId>
    <artifactId>slf4j-api</artifactId>
    <version>1.7.25</version>
</dependency>
<dependency>
    <groupId>org.slf4j</groupId>
    <artifactId>jcl-over-slf4j</artifactId>
    <version>1.7.25</version>
</dependency>
<dependency>
    <groupId>ch.qos.logback</groupId>
    <artifactId>logback-core</artifactId>
    <version>1.2.3</version>
</dependency>
```

```
<dependency>
    <groupId>ch.qos.logback</groupId>
    <artifactId>logback-classic</artifactId>
    <version>1.2.3</version>
</dependency>
</dependencies>

<build>
    <plugins>
        <plugin>
            <groupId>org.eclipse.jetty</groupId>
            <artifactId>jetty-maven-plugin</artifactId>
            <version>9.4.10.v20180503</version>
        </plugin>
    </plugins>
</build>
```

We add Spring Framework, Spring Security, JSP/JSTL, and the logging framework (SLF4J and Logback) dependencies. We will be using an embedded jetty server (look at the build section) to run our application.

Setting up LoginModule

LoginModule is responsible for authenticating a user. We will be creating our own LoginModule named JaasLoginModule and then implementing the login method. Being a sample application, our login logic is quite trivial. The LoginModule interface has to be implemented for you to write your own custom login module.

Create a class, JaasLoginModule.java (which implements LoginModule), and implement all the methods. In this class, we will be focusing on two important methods. In the initialize method, we get all the necessary information, such as username/password/subject, that is stored as field variables to be used in our main login method:

```
// Gather information and then use this in the login method
@Override
public void initialize(Subject subject, CallbackHandler callbackHandler,
Map<String,
            ?> sharedState, Map<String, ?> options) {
    this.subject = subject;

    NameCallback nameCallback = new NameCallback("Username:");
    PasswordCallback passwordCallback = new PasswordCallback("Password:",
false);
    try {
```

```
            callbackHandler.handle(new Callback[] { nameCallback,
    passwordCallback });
        } catch (IOException e) {
            e.printStackTrace();
        } catch (UnsupportedCallbackException e) {
            e.printStackTrace();
        }
        username = nameCallback.getName();
        password = new String(passwordCallback.getPassword());
    }
```

In the `login` method, we will log in using the values stored in the `initialize` method. In our case, if the hard-coded username/password is valid, set the principal in the subject:

```
// Code where actual login happens. Implement any logic as required by your
application
// In our sample we are just doing a hard-coded comparison of username and
password
@Override
public boolean login() throws LoginException {
    if (username == null || (username.equalsIgnoreCase("")) ||
        password == null || (password.equalsIgnoreCase(""))) {
        throw new LoginException("Username and password is mandatory.");
    } else if (username.equalsIgnoreCase("admin") &&
        password.equalsIgnoreCase("password")) {
        subject.getPrincipals().add(new JaasPrincipal(username));
        return true;
    } else if (username.equalsIgnoreCase("user") &&
        password.equalsIgnoreCase("password")) {
        subject.getPrincipals().add(new JaasPrincipal(username));
        return true;
    }
    return false;
}
```

Setting up a custom principal

We have created our own custom principal class by implementing the `java.security.Principal` interface. It's a very simple class in which we take in the username through a constructor and then use that to return in the `getName` method:

```
public class JaasPrincipal implements Principal, Serializable {
    private String username;
    public JaasPrincipal(String username) {
        this.username = username;
    }
```

```
@Override
public String getName() {
    return "Authenticated_"+this.username;
}
}
```

Setting up a custom AuthorityGranter

`AuthorityGranter` is entrusted to provide relevant roles to the authenticated user. We will be creating our own custom class by implementing `org.springframework.security.authentication.jaas.AuthorityGranter`:

```
public class JaasAuthorityGranter implements AuthorityGranter {
    @Override
    public Set<String> grant(Principal principal) {
        if (principal.getName().equalsIgnoreCase("Authenticated_admin")) {
            return Collections.singleton("ROLE_ADMIN");
        } else if (principal.getName().equalsIgnoreCase("Authenticated_user")) {
            return Collections.singleton("ROLE_USER");
        }
        return Collections.singleton("ROLE_USER");
    }
}
```

Being a sample implementation, in this class, we look at the logged in users username and grant a hard-coded role to it. In real-life applications, we would be doing something more serious in here by actually querying a database and then granting appropriate roles to the logged in user.

Configuration files

We need to have a number of configuration files (Java configuration) in our sample, most of which have been covered earlier. For the remaining files (yet to be covered), we will either run through them quickly or go into details when they are covered.

Application configuration

We don't have any application-specific configuration here but it's always good to have such a file in your application. We have `ApplicationConfig.java` as our application-level Java configuration (it doesn't have any content in it).

Spring MVC configuration

As shown in the following code, here we will be creating Spring MVC specific Java configurations (`SpringMVCConfig.java`):

```
@Configuration
@EnableWebMvc
@ComponentScan( basePackages = "com.packtpub")
public class SpringMVCConfig implements WebMvcConfigurer {
    @Override
    public void configureViewResolvers(ViewResolverRegistry registry) {
        registry.jsp().prefix("/WEB-INF/views/").suffix(".jsp");
    }
    @Override
    public void addViewControllers(ViewControllerRegistry registry) {
        registry.addViewController("/login");
    }
}
```

In this configuration, set the view's *prefix* and *suffix*. Make sure that your login view controller is added explicitly, as we don't have a route defined in our controller (we will see the controller later).

Spring Security configuration

This is a very important configuration example.

We will create an `AuthenticationProvider` bean. We will be using our custom `LoginModule` and then use `org.springframework.security.authentication.jaas.DefaultJaasAuthenticationProvider` to set things up. We then set this authentication provider as the global provider. Any request will pass through this provider (`SpringSecurityConfig.java`):

```
@Bean
DefaultJaasAuthenticationProvider jaasAuthenticationProvider() {
    AppConfigurationEntry appConfig = new
AppConfigurationEntry("com.packtpub.book.ch04.springsecurity.loginmodule.Ja
asLoginModule",
            AppConfigurationEntry.LoginModuleControlFlag.REQUIRED, new
HashMap());

    InMemoryConfiguration memoryConfig = new InMemoryConfiguration(new
AppConfigurationEntry[] { appConfig });

    DefaultJaasAuthenticationProvider def = new
DefaultJaasAuthenticationProvider();
```

```
        def.setConfiguration(memoryConfig);
        def.setAuthorityGranters(new AuthorityGranter[] {jaasAuthorityGranter});
        return def;
    }

    //We are configuring jaasAuthenticationProvider as our global
    AuthenticationProvider
    @Autowired
    public void configureGlobal(AuthenticationManagerBuilder auth) throws
    Exception {
        auth.authenticationProvider(jaasAuthenticationProvider());
    }
```

The next most important method is the `configure` method, in which we will make sure that we set the right path which need to be secured and we will also set up some important configurations:

```
    // Setting up our HTTP security
    @Override
    protected void configure(HttpSecurity http) throws Exception {

        // Setting up security
        http.authorizeRequests()
                .regexMatchers("/admin/.*").hasRole("ADMIN")
                .anyRequest().authenticated().and().httpBasic();

        // Setting our login page and to make it public
        http.formLogin().loginPage("/login").permitAll();
        // Logout configuration
        http.logout().logoutSuccessUrl("/");
        // Exception handling, for access denied
        http.exceptionHandling().accessDeniedPage("/noaccess");
    }
```

Controllers

We just have one controller in which we will configure all the routes
(`JaasController.java`):

```
    @Controller
    public class JaasController {
        @RequestMapping(value="/", method = RequestMethod.GET)
        public ModelAndView userPage() {
            ModelAndView modelAndView = new ModelAndView("user");
            return modelAndView;
        }
        @RequestMapping(value = "/admin/moresecured", method =
```

```
RequestMethod.GET)
    public ModelAndView adminPage(HttpServletRequest request) {
        ModelAndView modelAndView = new ModelAndView();
        modelAndView.setViewName("moresecured");
        return modelAndView;
    }
    @RequestMapping(value="/noaccess", method = RequestMethod.GET)
    public ModelAndView accessDenied() {
        ModelAndView modelAndView = new ModelAndView("noaccess");
        return modelAndView;
    }
}
```

Setting up pages

We have a few trivial pages. I don't want to paste the code in here, as it is quite self-explanatory:

- login.jsp: Our custom login page, which is used to collect username and password from the end user.
- user.jsp: The page that is set as root in the sample. After login, the user is navigated to this page. We just print the session ID and also the username to showcase the login.
- moresecured.jsp: This is just to showcase how the role of the user matters. This page can only be accessed by a user having the ADMIN role.
- noaccess.jsp: When the user doesn't have access to any page, this dummy page comes in for the user.

A full sample project can be found in the book's GitHub page within the *jetty-jaas-authentication* project.

Running the application

From the root of the project, execute the following command:

```
mvn jetty:run
```

Open a browser and navigate to http://localhost:8080. You will be provided with a dirty-looking login page. Enter username/password (admin/password or user/password) and you will be navigated to the root page (user.jsp).

This completes our JAAS example using Spring Security. As shown in Figure 8 above, JAAS can be used to achieve authentication using other protocols. One of the well-known mechanism is authentication using Kerberos protocol. Next brief section gives you a rough idea of how JAAS can be used to achieve Kerberos based authentication.

Kerberos

JAAS provides a number of built-in types of `LoginModule` and one of them is `rb5LoginModule`, which is used to authenticate users using the Kerberos protocol. So, indeed, JAAS methodology can be used to achieve Kerberos authentication within your Spring-based application with ease.

Let's get into some more important details about authentication.

Custom AuthenticationEntryPoint

A custom `AuthenticationEntryPoint` can be used to set necessary response headers, content-type, and so on before sending the response back to the client.

The `org.springframework.security.web.authentication.www.BasicAuthenticationEntryPoint` class is a built-in `AuthenticationEntryPoint` implementation, which will get invoked for basic authentication to commence. A custom entry point can be created by implementing the `org.springframework.security.web.AuthenticationEntryPoint` interface. The following is an example implementation:

```
@Component
public final class CustomAuthenticationEntryPoint implements
        AuthenticationEntryPoint {
    @Override
    public void commence(final HttpServletRequest request, final
            HttpServletResponse response, final AuthenticationException
        authException) throws IOException {
        response.sendError(HttpServletResponse.SC_UNAUTHORIZED,
"Unauthorized");
    }
}
```

When a client accesses resources without authentication, this entry point kicks in and throws a 401 status code (`Unauthorized`).

In the Spring Security Java configuration file, make sure that the `configure` method has this custom `AuthenticationEntryPoint` defined, as shown in the following code snippet:

```
@Override
protected void configure(HttpSecurity http) throws Exception {
    http
        .authorizeRequests()
        .antMatchers("/public").permitAll()
        .anyRequest().authenticated()
        .and()
        .httpBasic()
        .authenticationEntryPoint(customAuthenticationEntryPoint);
}
```

Multiple AuthenticationEntryPoint

Spring Security does allow you to configure multiple `AuthenticationEntryPoint` for your application, if needed.

Since Spring Security 3.0.2, `org.springframework.security.web.authentication.DelegatingAuthenticationEntryPoint` looks at all declared `AuthenticationEntryPoint` in the configurations and executes them.

Since Spring Security 5.x, we have `org.springframework.security.web.server.DelegatingServerAuthenticationEntryPoint`, which uses reactive data types and brings in asynchronous nature to its execution.

The `defaultAuthenticationEntryPointFor()` method in the Spring Security configuration can also be employed to set up multiple entry points looking at different URL matching (see the following code snippet):

```
@Override
protected void configure(HttpSecurity http) throws Exception {
    http
    .authorizeRequests()
        .antMatchers("/public").permitAll()
        .anyRequest().authenticated()
        .and()
        .httpBasic()
    .defaultAuthenticationEntryPointFor(
        loginUrlAuthenticationEntryPointUser(),
```

```
            new AntPathRequestMatcher("/secured/user/**"))
    .defaultAuthenticationEntryPointFor(
        loginUrlAuthenticationEntryPointAdmin(),
        new AntPathRequestMatcher("/secured/admin/**"));
}
@Bean
public AuthenticationEntryPoint loginUrlAuthenticationEntryPointUser(){
    return new LoginUrlAuthenticationEntryPoint("/userAuth");
}
@Bean
public AuthenticationEntryPoint loginUrlAuthenticationEntryPointAdmin(){
    return new LoginUrlAuthenticationEntryPoint("/adminAuth");
}
```

PasswordEncoder

Before Spring Security 5, the framework allowed only one PasswordEncoder throughout the application and also had weak password encoders such as MD5 and SHA. These encoders also didn't have dynamic salt, rather it had more static salt which had to be supplied. With Spring Security 5, there have been huge changes in this area and with the new version, the password encoding concept employs delegation and allows multiple password encoding within the same application. The password which has been encoded has a identifier prefixed to indicate what algorithm has been used (see the following example):

```
{bcrypt}$2y$10$zsUaFDpkjg01.JVipZhtFeOHpC2/LCH3yx6aNJpTNDOA8zDqhzgR6
```

This approach enables multiple encoding as needed within the application to be employed. If no identifier is mentioned, this means it uses the default encoder, which is StandardPasswordEncoder.

Once you decide on the password encoding, this can be used within the AuthenticationManager. One such example is the following code snippet:

```
@Autowired
public void configureGlobal(AuthenticationManagerBuilder auth) throws
Exception {
    auth
        .inMemoryAuthentication()
        .passwordEncoder(new StandardPasswordEncoder())
        .withUser("user")
.password("025baf3868bc8f785267d4aec1f02fa50809b7f715576198eda6466")
        .roles("USER");
}
```

Spring Security 5, as mentioned earlier, introduced a delegation approach by introducing `DelegationPasswordEncoder`. `DelegatingPasswordEncoder` has replaced `PasswordEncoder` and can be created by two approaches as follows:

- Approach 1:

```
PasswordEncoder passwordEncoder =
    PasswordEncoderFactories.createDelegatingPasswordEncoder();
passwordEncoder.setDefaultPasswordEncoderForMatches(new
BCryptPasswordEncoder());
```

- Approach 2:

```
String defaultEncode = "bcrypt";
Map encoders = new HashMap<>();
encoders.put(defaultEncode, new BCryptPasswordEncoder());
encoders.put("scrypt", new SCryptPasswordEncoder());
encoders.put("sha256", new StandardPasswordEncoder());

PasswordEncoder passwordEncoder =
    new DelegatingPasswordEncoder(defaultEncode, encoders);
```

`DelegatingPasswordEncoder` allows passwords to be validated against old encoding approaches and upgrades the password over a period of time without any hassle. This approach can be used to automatically upgrade passwords (old encoding to new encoding) as and when the user authenticates.

Salt

To make brute force attacks harder, while encoding we also can supply a random string. This random string is called **salt**. Salt text is included in `PasswordEncoder` as shown in the following code snippet:

```
auth
    .inMemoryAuthentication()
    .passwordEncoder(new StandardPasswordEncoder("random-text-salt"));
```

Custom filters

As explained earlier, Spring Security works on servlet filters. There are number of built-in servlet filters that do almost all the necessary functionalities. If needed, Spring Security does provide a mechanism to write your own custom filter and can be plugged in at the right point in the filter chain execution. Create your own filter by extending `org.springframework.web.filter.GenericFilterBean` as shown in the following code snippet:

```
public class NewLogicFilter extends GenericFilterBean {
    @Override
    public void doFilter(ServletRequest request, ServletResponse response,
            FilterChain chain) throws IOException, ServletException {
        // Custom logic
        chain.doFilter(request, response);
    }
}
```

Once you create your own filter, plug it into the filter chain in the Spring Security configuration file as follows:

```
@Configuration
public class SpringSecurityConfiguration extends
WebSecurityConfigurerAdapter {
    @Override
    protected void configure(HttpSecurity http) throws Exception {
        http
            .addFilterBefore(new NewLogicFilter(),
                BasicAuthenticationFilter.class);
    }
}
```

You can place the new filter before, after, or at a particular location in the filter chain. If you want to extend an existing filter, you have that provision as well.

Summary

In this chapter, we have covered two more authentication mechanisms, namely CAS and JAAS, supported by Spring Security, through hands-on coding examples. Again, we have used the sample application build as part of Chapter 2, *Deep Diving into Spring Security*, as a base to explain the working and implementation of other authentication mechanisms. We then covered some important concepts and the customization possible in Spring Security.

In this chapter, we intentionally didn't use reactive programming in our coding examples. This chapter was aimed at making you understand the core concepts of each CAS and JAAS authentication mechanism by making use of the familiar Spring Web MVC application framework. We will cover reactive programming in more detail in Chapter 5, *Integrating with Spring WebFlux*. We will start the next chapter by introducing you to Spring WebFlux and, in due course, implement Spring Security. While going through the main contents of Chapter 5, *Integrating with Spring WebFlux*, you will clearly understand that making the code examples in this chapter comply to reactive is quite easy.

Integrating with Spring WebFlux 5

One of the new features introduced as a part of Spring Framework 5 is the introduction of a new reactive web application framework, Spring WebFlux. WebFlux lives alongside the well-established web application framework Spring MVC. The book aims to introduce reactive parts of Spring Security in which Spring WebFlux is one of the core components.

Making your application reactive brings in an asynchronous nature to your application. Traditional Java applications used threads to achieve parallel and asynchronous nature to the application, however, usage of threads for a web application is not scalable and efficient in any manner.

This chapter starts by introducing you to the core differences between Spring MVC and Spring WebFlux. It then delves into the Spring Security module and how reactive aspects have been brought into it.

In this chapter, we will cover the following topics:

- Spring MVC versus WebFlux
- Reactive support in Spring 5
- Spring WebFlux
- Spring WebFlux authentication architecture
- Spring WebFlux authorization
- Sample project
- Customization

Spring MVC versus WebFlux

Spring WebFlux was brought in as part of Spring 5 to bring in a new alternative to existing Spring MVC. Spring WebFlux brings in non-blocking event loop style programming to provide asynchronicity.

Event loop was brought in and made famous by Node.js. Node.js was able to perform non-blocking operations using single-threaded JavaScript by offloading operations to the system kernel whenever possible. The kernel, being multithreaded, is able to do these offloaded operations and after successful execution notifies Node.js through callbacks. There is a constantly running process that checks the call stack (where operations are stacked which need to be executed) and keeps executing processes in **First In, First Out** (**FIFO**) manner. If the call stack is empty, it looks into the *Event Queue* for operations. It picks them up and then moves them to the call stack to be further picked for execution.

The following diagram shows what is in both web application frameworks:

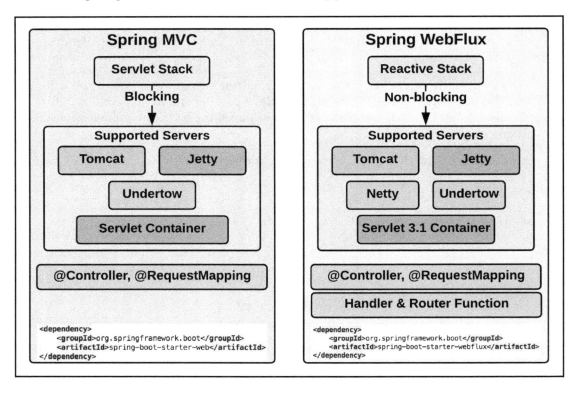

Figure 1: Spring MVC and Spring WebFlux

As shown in the preceding figure, Spring MVC is based on the Servlet API (works on thread pools) and Spring WebFlux is based on reactive streams (it works on an event loop mechanism). Both the frameworks, however, supports commonly used annotations such as `@Controller` and also support some well-known servers.

Let's see the workings of Spring MVC and Spring WebFlux side-by-side in the following diagram:

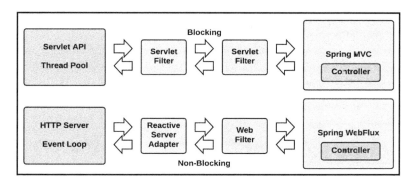

Figure 2: Working of Spring MVC and Spring WebFlux

As you can see, the fundamental difference between the working of the two frameworks is that Spring MVC is blocking and Spring WebFlux is non-blocking.

In Spring WebFlux, Servlet APIs behave as an adapter layer, enabling it to support both servlet containers such as **Tomcat** and **Jetty** and non-servlet runtimes such as **Undertow** and **Netty**.

Spring MVC comprises synchronous APIs (Filter, Servlet, and so on) and blocking I/O (InputStream, OutputStream, and so on) as against Spring WebFlux's asynchronous APIs (WebFilter, WebHandler, and so on) and non-blocking I/O (Reactor Mono for *0..1* elements and Rector Flux for *0..N* elements).

Spring WebFlux supports various asynchronous and Reactive APIs, namely Java 9 Flow API, RxJava, Reactor, and Akka Streams. By default, it uses Spring's very own reactive framework, Reactor, and it does do its job quite well:

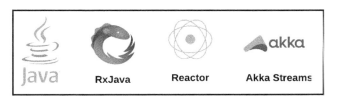

Figure 3: Spring WebFlux reactive API support

As mentioned earlier, Spring WebFlux was brought in as an alternative to Spring MVC. It doesn't mean in any way that Spring MVC is deprecated. Applications written in Spring MVC can continue running on the same stack without any migration to Spring WebFlux. If needs be, we can bring in reactive coding practices to an existing Spring MVC application by running a reactive client to make calls to remote services.

Now that we have seen the features of the two web application frameworks in Spring, the next section will give an idea as to when to choose what framework while building your application.

When to choose what?

Reactive programming is quite good but that doesn't mean that we have to go reactive for every application. Along the same lines, not all the applications are a good fit for Spring WebFlux. Choose the framework by looking at the requirements and how these frameworks can solve them. If an application is working fine with Spring MVC as a framework, there is no need to port that to Spring WebFlux. In fact, as mentioned earlier, good parts of reactive can be brought into Spring MVC if needs be without much trouble.

Also, if the application already has blocking dependencies (JDBC, LDAP, and so on), then it's better to stick with Spring MVC as there would be complications bringing in reactive concepts. Even if we bring in reactive concepts, many parts of the application are in blocking mode, which will prevent taking full advantage of such a programming paradigm.

Adopt Spring WebFlux if your application deals with streams of data (input and output). Also, consider this as the web application choice if scalability and performance is of utmost importance. By their sheer nature, asynchronous and non-blocking, these applications would be performant compared to synchronous and blocking. Being asynchronous, they can deal with latencies and are more scalable.

Reactive support in Spring 5

Spring Framework 5 has extensive support for a reactive programming paradigm. Many of the modules have embraced this concept with both hands and are making it a first-class citizen. The following diagram summarizes the Spring 5 support of reactive:

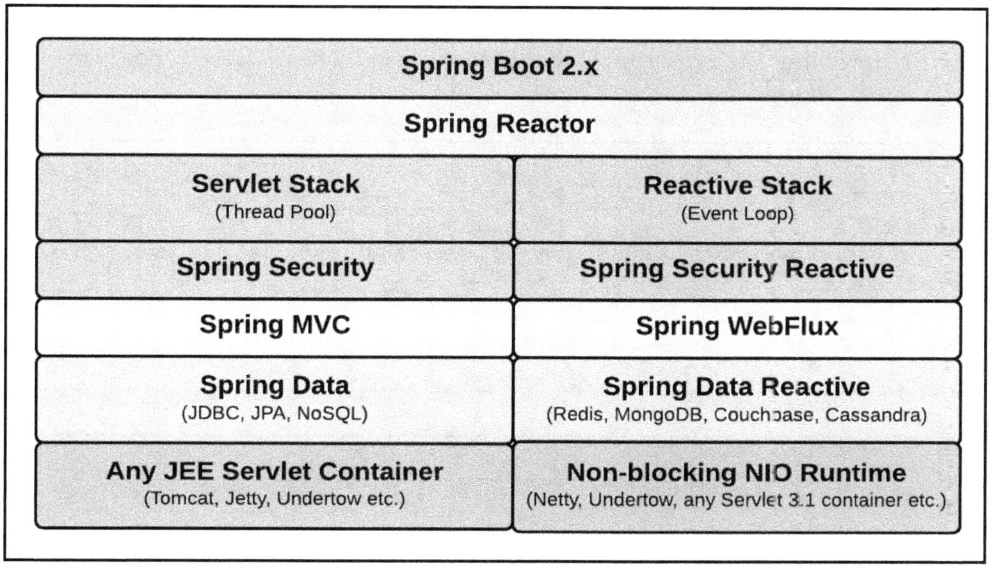

Figure 4: Spring 5 and reactive support

Spring WebFlux module is a full-fledged web application framework built on top of a reactive programming paradigm (it uses Reactor and RxJava). Some of the early adopters of reactive programming in the Spring/Java ecosystem were **Spring Data**, **Spring Security**, and **Thymeleaf**. Spring Security has a number of features that supports reactive programming.

Spring Data has reactive support for Redis, MongoDB, Couchbase, and Cassandra. It also supports infinite streams (records emitted one by one in the form of a stream) from the database with `@Tailable`. JDBC inherently is blocking in nature, because of which, Spring Data JPA is blocking and cannot be made reactive.

Reactive in Spring MVC

Even though Spring MVC is inherently blocking, some aspects can be made reactive by using reactive programming capabilities available as part of Spring 5.

In a Spring MVC controller, you can employ reactive types, `Flux` and `Mono`, as shown in the following diagram. The only rule is that you can use these reactive types only as the controller's return values:

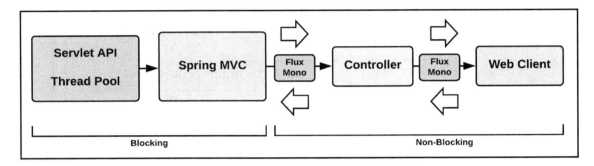

Figure 5: Spring MVC becoming non-blocking with usage of reactive types

Spring MVC annotations such as `@Controller`, `@RequestMapping`, and so on are also supported in Spring WebFlux. So converting a Spring MVC web application to Spring WebFlux can be done over a period of time in a slow-paced manner.

Spring WebFlux

In this section, we will go into a bit more detail on Spring WebFlux. There are two (programming model) ways by which Spring WebFlux can be used. They are as follows:

- **Using annotations**: By using annotations such as `@Controller` similar to how it is been done in Spring MVC
- **Using functional style**: By using routing and handling with Java Lambdas

The following code shows the annotation-based style of using Spring WebFlux. We will be going through the entire code sample in subsequent sections in this chapter. This section, however, is aimed at giving an introduction before we delve deeper:

```
@RestController
@RequestMapping(value="/api/movie")
public class MovieAPI {
    @GetMapping("/")
    public Flux(Movie) getMovies() {
        //Logic of getting all movies
    }
    @GetMapping("/{id}")
    public Mono<Movie> getMovie(@PathVariable Long id) {
```

```
        //Logic for getting a specific movie
    }
    @PostMapping("/post")
    public Mono<ResponseEntity<String>> createMovie(@RequestBody Movie
movie) {
        // Logic for creating movie
    }
}
```

The functional-style programming model of Spring WebFlux uses two fundamental components:

- HandlerFunction: Entrusted to handle an HTTP request. Equivalent to @Controller handler methods we have seen in our previous code snippet.
- RouterFunction: Entrusted to route an HTTP request. Equivalent to @RequestMapping in annotation-based.

HandlerFunction

HandlerFunction accepts a ServerRequest object and returns Mono<ServerResponse>. Both ServerRequest and ServerResponse objects are immutable and fully reactive, built on top of Reactor.

ServerRequest exposes the body as Mono or Flux. Traditionally, BodyExtractor is used to achieve this. However, it also has utility methods which exposes these objects as shown in the following code. ServerRequest also gives access to all HTTP request elements, such as method, URI, and query string parameters:

```
Mono<String> helloWorld = request.body(BodyExtractors.toMono(String.class);
Mono<String> helloWorldUtil = request.bodyToMono(String.class);

Flux<Person> movie = request.body(BodyExtractors.toFlux(Movie.class);
Flux<Person> movieUtil = request.bodyToFlux(Movie.class);
```

The ServerResponse object gives you access to various HTTP responses. The ServerResponse object can be created by using a builder, which allows setting response status and response headers. It also allows you to set the response body:

```
Mono<Movie> movie = ...
ServerResponse.ok().contentType(MediaType.APPLICATION_JSON).body(movie);
```

`HandlerFunction` can be created using a Lambda function as in the following code and return `ServerResponse` with status 200 OK and with a body based on a `String`:

```
HandlerFunction<ServerResponse> handlerFunction =
  request -> ServerResponse.ok().body(fromObject("Sample
HandlerFunction"));
```

It is recommended to group all `HandlerFunction` objects into a single class having multiple methods, each handling a specific function, as shown in the following code snippet:

```
public class MovieHandler {
    public Mono<ServerResponse> listMovies(ServerRequest request) {
        // Logic that returns all Movies objects
    }
    public Mono<ServerResponse> createMovie(ServerRequest request) {
        // Logic that returns creates Movie object in the request object
    }
    public Mono<ServerResponse> getMovie(ServerRequest request) {
        // Logic that returns one Movie object
    }
    //.. More methods as needed
}
```

RouterFunction

Incoming requests are intercepted by `RouterFunction`, and, according to the configured route, it is navigated to the right `HandlerFunction`. If the route is matched; `RouterFunction` takes in `ServerRequest` and returns back `Mono<HandlerFunction>`. If not, empty `Mono` is returned.

`RouterFunction` is created as shown in the following code snippet:

```
RouterFunctions.route(RequestPredicate, HandlerFunction)
```

`RequestPredicate` is a utility class that has predefined matching patterns for most of the common use cases, such as matching based on path, content type, HTTP method, and so on. An example code snippet for `RouterFunction` is as follows:

```
RouterFunction<ServerResponse> routeFunctionSample =
    RouterFunctions.route(RequestPredicates.path("/sample-route"),
    request -> Response.ok().body(fromObject("Sample Route")));
```

Multiple `RouterFunction` objects can be composed by invoking the following method:

```
RouterFunction.and(RouterFunction)
```

There is also a convenient method, as follows, which is a combination of the `RouterFunction.and()` and `RouterFunctions.route()` methods:

```
RouterFunction.andRoute(RequestPredicate, HandlerFunction)
```

The `RouterFunction` for the previous `HandlerFunction` is as follows:

```
RouterFunction<ServerResponse> movieRoutes =
    route(GET("/movie/{id}").and(accept(APPLICATION_JSON)),
handler::getMovie)
    .andRoute(GET("/movie").and(accept(APPLICATION_JSON)),
handler::listMovies)
    .andRoute(POST("/movie").and(contentType(APPLICATION_JSON)),
handler::createMovie);
```

Spring WebFlux server support

Spring Webflux supports a number of servers, as follows:

- Netty
- Jetty
- Tomcat
- Undertow
- Servlet 3.1+ containers

Spring Boot 2+ uses Netty by default, when the web application framework selected is Spring WebFlux.

The `RouterFunction` created can be run on any of the servers listed previously. To do that, `RouterFunction` needs to be converted to `HttpHandler`, using the following method:

```
RouterFunctions.toHttpHandler(RouterFunction)
```

If you want to run the previously created `RouterFunction` in Netty, the following code snippet can be used:

```
HttpHandler httpHandler = RouterFunctions.toHttpHandler(movieRoutes);
ReactorHttpHandlerAdapter reactorAdapter = new
ReactorHttpHandlerAdapter(httpHandler);
```

```
HttpServer server = HttpServer.create(HOST, PORT);
server.newHandler(reactorAdapter).block();
```

When we look at our sample application in subsequent sections of this chapter, we will look at code for other Spring WebFlux supported servers.

Reactive WebClient

Spring WebFlux includes a reactive client named WebClient, enabling us to perform HTTP requests in a non-blocking manner and to use reactive streams. WebClient can be used as an alternative to RestTemplate, which is used more traditionally. WebClient exposes reactive ClientHttpRequest and ClientHttpResponse objects. The bodies of these objects consist of reactive Flux<DataBuffer>, as opposed to traditional blocking stream implementation (InputStream and OutputStream).

Create an instance of WebClient, perform a request, and then handle the response. The following is a code snippet showing the WebClient usage:

```
WebClient client = WebClient.create("http://any-domain.com");
Mono<Movie> movie = client.get()
        .url("/movie/{id}", 1L)
        .accept(APPLICATION_JSON)
        .exchange(request)
        .then(response -> response.bodyToMono(Movie.class));
```

WebClient can be used from within both Spring MVC and Spring WebFlux web applications. RestTemplate usage can quite easily be swapped with WebClient, making use of the reactive advantages it provides.

In our sample project, we will cover the concepts and functionality of WebClient, using an example.

Reactive WebTestClient

Similar to WebClient, Spring WebFlux provides you with a non-blocking, reactive client named WebTestClient, to test your reactive APIs on your server. It has utilities that make testing these APIs easily in a test environment setup. WebTestClient can connect to any of the servers, as detailed earlier over an HTTP connection and execute necessary tests. However, the client has the capability of running the tests with and without a running server.

`WebTestClient` also has a number of utilities to verify the response produced by executing these server side APIs. It can quite easily bind itself to the WebFlux web application and mock necessary request and response objects to ascertain the API's functional aspects. `WebTestClient` can mutate the headers as needed, to simulate the desired test environment. You can get an instance of `WebTestClient` for your entire application (by using the `WebTestClient.bindToApplicationContext` method), or you can restrict it to specific controller (using the `WebTextClient.bindToController` method), `RouterFunction` (using the `WebTestClient.bindToRouterFunction` method), and so on.

We will see a detailed example of how `WebTestClient` works in a subsequent hands-on section (The *Sample project* section, under the *Testing (WebTestClient)* sub-section).

Reactive WebSocket

Spring WebFlux includes a reactive `WebSocket` client and server support based on the Java WebSocket API.

On the server, create `WebSocketHandlerAdapter`, and then map each of those handlers to the URL. Since we don't cover `WebSocket` in our sample application, let's go into a bit more detail:

```
public class MovieWebSocketHandler implements WebSocketHandler {
    @Override
    public Mono<Void> handle(WebSocketSession session) {
        // ...
    }
}
```

The `handle()` method takes in the `WebSocketSession` object and returns `Mono<Void>` when the handling of session is complete. `WebSocketSession` handles inbound and outbound messages using the `Flux<WebSocketMessage> receive()` and `Mono<Void> send(Publisher<WebSocketMessage>)` methods, respectively.

In the web application Java configuration, declare a bean for `WebSocketHandlerAcpater` and create another bean to map the URL to the appropriate `WebSocketHandler`, as shown in the following code snippet:

```
@Configuration
static class WebApplicationConfig {
    @Bean
    public HandlerMapping webSockerHandlerMapping() {
        Map<String, WebSocketHandler> map = new HashMap<>();
```

```
        map.put("/movie", new MovieWebSocketHandler());

        SimpleUrlHandlerMapping mapping = new SimpleUrlHandlerMapping();
        mapping.setUrlMap(map);
        return mapping;
    }
    @Bean
    public WebSocketHandlerAdapter handlerAdapter() {
        return new WebSocketHandlerAdapter();
    }
}
```

Spring WebFlux also provides `WebSocketClient` and has abstractions for all of the web servers discussed earlier, such as Netty, Jetty, and so on. Use appropriate server abstractions and create the client, as shown in the following code snippet:

```
WebSocketClient client = new ReactorNettyWebSocketClient();
URI url = new URI("ws://localhost:8080/movie");
client.execute(url, session ->
        session.receive()
            .doOnNext(System.out::println)
            .then());
```

In the client code, we can now subscribe to the `WebSocket`, endpoint and listen to messages and do the needful (basic `WebSocket` implementation). The code snippet for such a client on the frontend is as follows:

```
<script>
    var clientWebSocket = new WebSocket("ws://localhost:8080/movie");
    clientWebSocket.onopen = function() {
        // Logic as needed
    }
    clientWebSocket.onclose = function(error) {
        // Logic as needed
    }
    clientWebSocket.onerror = function(error) {
        // Logic as needed
    }
    clientWebSocket.onmessage = function(error) {
        // Logic as needed
    }
</script>
```

To keep the chapter focused and concise, we will not go over `WebSocket` security provided by Spring Security. In the last chapter of this book, we will quickly cover the `WebSocket` security, using an example.

Spring WebFlux authentication architecture

With the core Spring WebFlux concepts covered, we will now get into the crux of this chapter; introducing you to Spring Security for Spring WebFlux based reactive web applications.

As seen earlier, Spring Security in Spring MVC web applications is based on ServletFilter, and for Spring WebFlux, it is based on WebFilter:

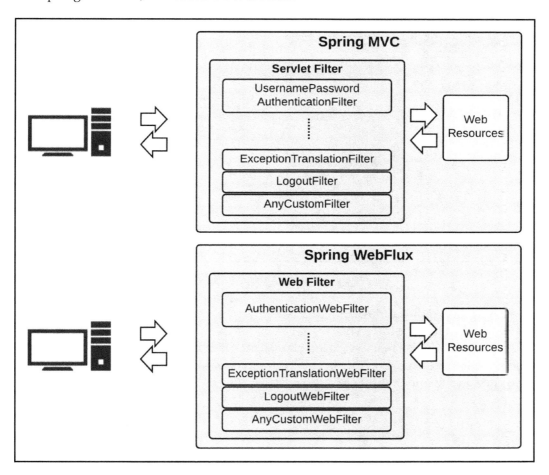

Figure 6: Spring MVC and Spring WebFlux authentication approach

We saw Spring Security in detail in Spring MVC web applications in previous chapters. We will now look at the inner details of Spring Security authentication for a Spring WebFlux based web application. The following diagram shows the interaction of various classes when an authentication process kicks in for a WebFlux application:

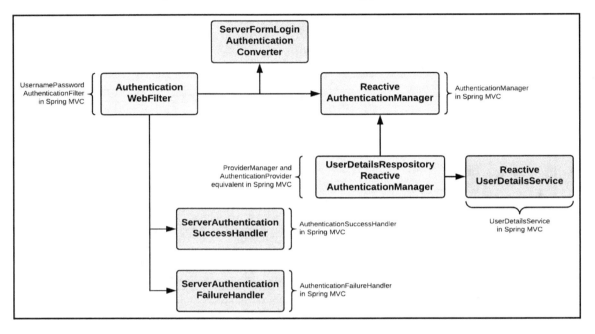

Figure 7: Spring WebFlux authentication architecture

The preceding diagram is quite self-explanatory, and is very similar to what you saw earlier for Spring MVC. The core difference is that `ServletFilter` is now replaced with `WebFilter`, and we have reactive-based classes for other blocking classes in Spring MVC. However, the core concepts of Spring Security remain intact with `WebFilter` dealing with many aspects in the initial authentication process; the core authentication is handled by `ReactiveAuthenticationManager` and related classes.

Spring WebFlux authorization

Similar to authentication, the core concepts, in regard to authorization remains similar to what we have seen earlier in Spring MVC. However, the classes performing the operation have changed, and are, reactive and non-blocking. The following diagram shows the authorization-related main classes and their interactions in a Spring WebFlux application:

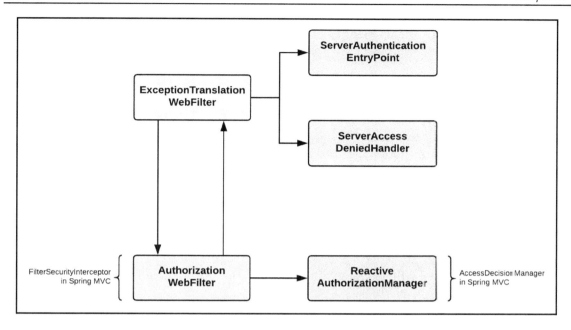

Figure 8: Authorization-related classes in a Spring WebFlux application

As we all know by now, Spring WebFlux security works on `WebFilter`, and `AuthorizationWebFilter` intercepts the request and uses `ReactiveAuthorizationManager` to check whether the `Authentication` object has access to a protected resource. `ReactiveAuthorizationManager` has two methods, namely, `check` (checks whether access is granted to an `Authentication` object) and `verify` (checks whether access has to be granted for an `Authentication` object). In the event of any exception, `ExceptionTranslationWebFilter` takes care of handling this by following the appropriate paths.

Sample project

Enough explanation; it's time to get our hands dirty with actual code. In this section, we will create a movie catalog site with integrated Spring Security. We will be using reactive concepts throughout and will use form-based login. We will start with hardcoded users and then see how we can look at a persistent user store to authenticate the users against. We will then into testing in more detail and finally look at some customizations that we can bring to Spring Security pages. Finally, we will touch base on authorization aspects and close the sample application.

WebFlux project setup

We will create a basic WebFlux-based web application first, and will slowly add other features, including security, in it. The whole code is available in our book's GitHub page, under the chapter's folder, namely `spring-boot-webflux`.

I am using IntelliJ as my IDE, and since we are using *Lombok library* (annotation `preprocessor`), make sure to enable the Lombok plugin, so as to generate appropriate boilerplate code for your model. Our project is kept quite simple, and does the function of movie management (the movie CRUD operation).

Maven setup

Using Spring Initializr for generating a Spring WebFlux project is really easy. But for us to get a handle on the various aspects of a WebFlux application, we will build aspect by ourselves. However, we will be using Spring Boot to run our application.

We will create a maven project, and will then add the following main dependencies (to make the code shorter, only important dependencies are shown in the following code) to our pom.xml:

```xml
<!--Spring Framework and Spring Boot-->
<dependency>
  <groupId>org.springframework.boot</groupId>
  <artifactId>spring-boot-starter-webflux</artifactId>
</dependency>
<!--JSON-->
<dependency>
...
</dependency>
<!--Logging-->
<dependency>
...
</dependency>
<!--Testing-->
<dependency>
...
</dependency>
```

We will include snapshot repositories for both the library and plugin dependencies. Finally, we will add the all-important maven plugin for our Spring Boot, as follows:

```xml
<build>
  <plugins>
    <plugin>
```

```
            <groupId>org.springframework.boot</groupId>
            <artifactId>spring-boot-maven-plugin</artifactId>
        </plugin>
    </plugins>
</build>
```

Configuration class

Even though we are going to use default configurations as much as possible, we will still
have separate configuration classes for various components. In our project, we are building
a basic WebFlux application, thus we have only one configuration class.

The SpringWebFluxConfig class

The main configuration class for a Spring WebFlux web application is achieved by this
class:

```
@Configuration
@EnableWebFlux
@ComponentScan
public class SpringWebFluxConfig {
  // ...
}
```

We have an empty class with just some very important annotations as shown in the
preceding code. @EnableWebFlux makes the application reactive and makes it WebFlux.

Repository

We will be using hardcoded movies as our data structure for this sample and will write
methods in a reactive way, to expose methods in our repository class. These methods can
be used to manipulate the data structure of the movies. Our repository class is a
conventional one, but the right data structures, in the form of Mono and Flux, aid in
bringing a reactive nature to the application:

```
@Repository
public class MovieRepositoryImpl implements MovieRepository {
    private Map<Long, Movie> movies = new HashMap<Long, Movie>();

    @PostConstruct
    public void initIt() throws Exception {
      movies.put(Long.valueOf(1), new Movie(Long.valueOf(1), "Moonlight",
        "Drama"));
      movies.put(Long.valueOf(2), new Movie(Long.valueOf(2), "Dunkirk",
```

```
        "Drama/Thriller"));
    movies.put(Long.valueOf(3), new Movie(Long.valueOf(3), "Get Out",
        "Mystery/Thriller"));
    movies.put(Long.valueOf(4), new Movie(Long.valueOf(4), "The Shape of
        Water", "Drama/Thriller"));
    }
    @Override
    public Mono<Movie> getMovieById(Long id) {
        return Mono.just(movies.get(id));
    }
    //...Other methods
}
```

The class is just a snippet extracted from the class, and shows only one method (getMovieById). As always, our class implements an interface (MovieRepository), and this reference will be used in other parts of the application (using Spring's Dependency Injection capability).

Handler and router

As detailed previously, we have two approaches, namely **functional-based** and **annotation-based**, for implementing a WebFlux application. Annotation-based is similar to Spring MVC, and because of this, we will be using functional-based approach in our sample application:

```
@Component
public class MovieHandler {
    private final MovieRepository movieRepository;

    public MovieHandler(MovieRepository movieRepository) {
        this.movieRepository = movieRepository;
    }
    public Mono<ServerResponse> listMovies(ServerRequest request) {
        // fetch all Movies from repository
        Flux<Movie> movies = movieRepository.listMovies();
        // build response
        return
            ServerResponse.ok().contentType(MediaType.APPLICATION_JSON)
            .body(movies, Movie.class);
    }
    //...Other methods
}
```

The class is quite straightforward and uses a repository class for data structure query and manipulation. Each method accomplishes the functionality, and finally returns `Mono<ServerResponse>`. Another important aspect of WebFlux in functional-based programming is the routing configuration class, as follows:

```
@Configuration
public class RouterConfig {

    @Bean
    public RouterFunction<ServerResponse> routerFunction1(MovieHandler
        movieHandler) {
      return
        route(GET("/").and(accept(MediaType.APPLICATION_JSON)),
            movieHandler::listMovies)
.andRoute(GET("/api/movie").and(accept(MediaType.APPLICATION_JSON)),
            movieHandler::listMovies)
.andRoute(GET("/api/movie/{id}").and(accept(MediaType.APPLICATION_JSON)),
            movieHandler::getMovieById)
.andRoute(POST("/api/movie").and(accept(MediaType.APPLICATION_JSON)),
            movieHandler::saveMovie)
.andRoute(PUT("/api/movie/{id}").and(accept(MediaType.APPLICATION_JSON)),
            movieHandler::putMovie)
        .andRoute(DELETE("/api/movie/{id}")
            .and(accept(MediaType.APPLICATION_JSON)),
movieHandler::deleteMovie);
    }
}
```

This is the class that looks at the request and routes it to the appropriate handler method. In your application, you can have any number of router configuration files.

Bootstrap application

Our sample application uses Spring Boot. Spring WebFlux runs on a Reactor Netty server within Spring Boot by default. Our Spring Boot class is very basic and is as follows:

```
@SpringBootApplication
public class Run {
  public static void main(String[] args) {
      SpringApplication.run(Run.class, args);
  }
}
```

You can run the application on any other server, apart from Spring Boot, and it is quite easy to achieve. We have a separate project named `spring-boot-tomcat-webflux` that runs on Spring Boot, but rather than running on Reactor Netty, it runs on a Tomcat server.

No change is required in any part of the code, apart from `pom.xml`:

```xml
<!--Spring Framework and Spring Boot-->
<dependency>
    <groupId>org.springframework.boot</groupId>
    <artifactId>spring-boot-starter-webflux</artifactId>
    <exclusions>
        <exclusion>
            <groupId>org.springframework.boot</groupId>
            <artifactId>spring-boot-starter-reactor-netty</artifactId>
        </exclusion>
    </exclusions>
</dependency>
<!--Explicit Tomcat dependency-->
<dependency>
    <groupId>org.springframework.boot</groupId>
    <artifactId>spring-boot-starter-tomcat</artifactId>
</dependency>
```

From the `spring-boot-starter-webflux` artifact, exclude Reactor Netty. Thereafter, explicitly add the Tomcat dependency, `spring-boot-starter-tomcat`. The rest of the `pom.xml` is kept intact. For other server runtimes, such as Undertow, Jetty, and so on, the approach is similar to the one detailed here.

Running the application

Now, for the most important part: running the application that we built. As it is a Spring Boot application, execute the default command as follows:

```
mvn spring-boot:run
```

Once the server has started (default Rector Netty or Tomcat), open a browser and navigate to `localhost:8080/movies`. We have created default routing to point to "list all movies" endpoint and if all went well, you should see the JSON which shows all the hardcoded movies in our repository class.

In this section, we have created a sample Spring WebFlux movie application. We will add the all important security to this application in the next section.

Adding security

To separate from what we have achieved up until now, we will have a separate project, `spring-boot-security-webflux` (the same as `spring-boot-webflux`). In it we will build all the security aspects.

Configuration classes

We will be creating a new configuration class for Spring Security: `SpringSecurityWebFluxConfig`. Firstly, we will annotate the class with the most important annatation: `@EnableWebFluxSecurity`. This instructs it to enable Spring Security for WebFlux web applications. In the configuration class, we will look at two important beans, as follows.

The UserDetailsService bean

We will use hardcoded user details, against which we will authenticate. This is not how it has to be done for a production-ready application, but for simplicity and to explain the concepts, let's take this shortcut:

```
@Bean
public MapReactiveUserDetailsService userDetailsRepositcry() {
    UserDetails user = User.withUsername("user")
        .password("{noop}password").roles("USER").build();
    UserDetails admin = User.withUsername("admin")
        .password("{noop}password").roles("USER","ADMIN").build();
    return new MapReactiveUserDetailsService(user, admin);
}
```

The bean returns the reactive user details service, containing hardcoded credentials for two users; one a normal user and the other an admin.

The SpringSecurityFilterChain bean

This is the bean where we actually specify the Spring Security configuration:

```
@Bean
SecurityWebFilterChain springWebFilterChain(ServerHttpSecurity http)
    throws Exception {
    return http
    .authorizeExchange()
    .pathMatchers(HttpMethod.GET, "/api/movie/**").hasRole("USER")
    .pathMatchers(HttpMethod.POST, "/api/movie/**").hasRole("ADMIN")
    .anyExchange().authenticated()
```

```
        .and().formLogin()
        .and().build();
}
```

Similar to what we saw earlier, in the Spring MVC application earlier, we match URL patterns and specify the role that is needed to access it. We are configuring the login method as a form in which the user will be shown the default login form by Spring Security.

Running the application

Execute the following command:

```
mvn spring-boot:run
```

When the server starts up, you have two ways in which you can test the application, as follows.

CURL

Open your favorite Command Prompt and execute the following command:

```
curl http://localhost:8080/ -v
```

You will be redirected to the `http://localhost:8080/login` page. Your entire application is secured and without logging in, you will not be able to access any content. With form login as the method, you won't be able to test it using `curl`. Let's change the login method from form (`formLogin`) to basic (`httpBasic`) in the Spring Security configuration (the `springWebFilterChain` bean). Now, execute the following command:

```
curl http://localhost:8080/api/movie -v -u admin:password
```

You should now see the raw JSON displaying all of the hardcoded movies. Use other common CURL commands, as follows, to test other endpoints:

```
curl http://localhost:8080/api/movie/1 -v -u admin:password
```

Browser

Let's put the login method back to form, and then open a browser and navigate to `http://localhost:8080`. You will be navigated to the default Spring Security login page. Enter the username as `admin` and the password as `password`, and click on **Sign in**:

Figure 9: Default Spring Security login form

After successfully logging in, you will be navigated to the list all movies endpoint, as follows:

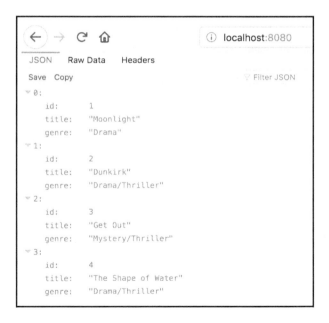

Figure 10: List all movies default home page after login

WebClient

On the book's GitHub page, we have a separate project (`spring-boot-security-webclient-webflux`), in which you can see the entire code that will be detailed in this section.

Maven setup

Create a base maven project and add the following main dependency to your `pom.xml` file:

```
<!--Spring Framework and Spring Boot-->
<dependency>
  <groupId>org.springframework.boot</groupId>
  <artifactId>spring-boot-starter-webflux</artifactId>
</dependency>
```

Now, add other dependencies, as well as the default Spring Boot build section.

Creating a WebClient instance

A `WebClient` instance can be created by using the `create()` method, or by using the `builder()` method. In our sample, we have used the `builder()` method, as follows:

```
@Service
public class WebClientTestImpl implements WebClientTestInterface {
    private final WebClient webClient;
    public WebClientTestImpl(WebClient.Builder webClientBuilder) {
        this.webClient = webClientBuilder.defaultHeader(HttpHeaders.ACCEPT,
        MediaType.APPLICATION_JSON_VALUE)
            .baseUrl("http://localhost:8080/api/movie").build();
    }
    //...Other methods
}
```

We will be using all of the endpoints that we have created earlier in our base Spring WebFlux project, and will be accessing them using the `WebClient`.

Use the `create()` method to create an instance of `WebClient`, as follows:

```
WebClient webClient = WebClient.create();
```

If you have a base URL, `WebClient` can be created as follows:

```
WebClient webClient = WebClient.create("http://localhost:8080/api/movie");
```

The `builder()` method provides bunch of utility methods, such as filters, setting headers, setting cookies, and so on. In our example, we have set some default headers and have also set the base URL.

Handling errors

A `WebClient` instance allows you to handle errors (the `WebClientTestImpl` class) in the `listMovies()` method, as follows:

```
@Override
public Flux<Movie> listMovies() {
    return webClient.get().uri("/")
        .retrieve()
        .onStatus(HttpStatus::is4xxClientError, clientResponse ->
            Mono.error(new SampleException())
        )
        .onStatus(HttpStatus::is5xxServerError, clientResponse ->
            Mono.error(new SampleException())
        )
        .bodyToFlux(Movie.class);
}
```

`SampleException` is a custom exception class that we created by extending the `Exception` class. We are handling 4xx and 5xx errors, and, when encountered, it sends the custom exception as response.

Sending requests and retrieving responses

The `retrieve()` method is a simple method, using which the response body can be retrieved. If you want to have more control over returned responses, the `exchange()` method can be used to retrieve the response. We have used both of the methods in our sample application; the code snippets for the two methods in the `WebClientTestImpl` class are as follows:

```
@Override
public Mono<Movie> getMovieById(Long id)
    return this.webClient.get().uri("/{id}", id)
            .retrieve().bodyToMono(Movie.class);
}
@Override
```

```
public Mono<Movie> saveMovie(Movie movie) {
   return webClient.post().uri("/")
           .body(BodyInserters.fromObject(movie))
           .exchange().flatMap( clientResponse ->
              clientResponse.bodyToMono(Movie.class) );
}
```

In the first method, we execute a GET method on the URI `http://localhost:8080/api/movie/{id}`, use the `retrieve()` method, and then convert into `Mono`.

In the second method, we execute a POST method on the URL `http://localhost:8080/api/movie`, use the `exchange()` method, and use the `flatMap()` method to create the response.

Running and testing the application

We will be using the same movie model in this sample project. Since this is the only class that we need from our previous sample application, we will copy the class here. In an ideal scenario, we would have a JAR file containing all common classes, and it can be included in our `pom.xml` file.

Create the `Run` class (as seen earlier) and call the `WebClient` methods. The code snippet for one of the methods is as follows:

```
@SpringBootApplication
public class Run implements CommandLineRunner {
  @Autowired
  WebClientTestInterface webClient;
  public static void main(String[] args) {
      SpringApplication.run(Run.class, args);
  }
  @Override
  public void run(String... args) throws Exception {
      // get all movies
      System.out.println("Get All Movies");
      webClient.listMovies().subscribe(System.out::println);
      Thread.sleep(3000);
      ... Other methods
  }
  //... Other WebClient methods getting called
}
```

After executing each `WebClient` call, we will sleep for three seconds. Since `WebClient` methods emit reactive types (`Mono` or `Flux`), you have to subscribe, as shown in the preceding code.

Start the `spring-boot-webflux` project, exposing the endpoints, which we will test by using `WebClient` in this project.

Make sure that your application's default port is changed in your `application.properties` file by including the following entry:

```
server.port=8081
```

Start the application by executing the Spring Boot command, as follows:

```
mvn spring-boot:run
```

If all goes well, you should see the output in the server console, as follows:

```
2018-06-03 20:25:47.372  INFO 23011 --- [ctor-http-nio-1] r.ipc.netty.tcp.BlockingNettyContext      : Started HttpServer on /0:0:0:0:0:0:0:0:8081
2018-06-03 20:25:47.373  INFO 23011 --- [           main] o.s.b.web.embedded.netty.NettyWebServer   : Netty started on port(s): 8081
2018-06-03 20:25:47.379  INFO 23011 --- [           main] c.packtpub.book.ch02.springsecurity.Run   : Started Run in 2.19 seconds (JVM running for 5.431)
Get All Movies
Movie(id=1, title=Moonlight, genre=Drama)
Movie(id=2, title=Dunkirk, genre=Drama/Thriller)
Movie(id=3, title=Get Out, genre=Mystery/Thriller)
Movie(id=4, title=The Shape of Water, genre=Drama/Thriller)
Get a Movie with id = 1
Movie(id=1, title=Moonlight, genre=Drama)
Save a Movie
Update a Movie
Movie(id=3, title=Black Panther, genre=Fantasy/Science)
Delete a Movie with id = 2
Get All Movies again
Movie(id=1, title=Moonlight, genre=Drama)
Movie(id=3, title=Get Out, genre=Mystery/Thriller)
Movie(id=4, title=The Shape of Water, genre=Drama/Thriller)
```

Figure 11: WebClient test execution

Unit testing (WebTestClient)

In our base `spring-boot-webflux` project, we have written test cases using `WebTestClient`. We have two test cases: one to get all movies, and other to save movie.

Maven dependency

Make sure that you have the following dependencies in your pom.xml file:

```
<!--Testing-->
<dependency>
  <groupId>junit</groupId>
  <artifactId>junit</artifactId>
  <scope>test</scope>
</dependency>
<dependency>
  <groupId>org.springframework</groupId>
  <artifactId>spring-test</artifactId>
  <scope>test</scope>
</dependency>
<dependency>
  <groupId>org.skyscreamer</groupId>
  <artifactId>jsonassert</artifactId>
  <scope>test</scope>
</dependency>
<dependency>
  <groupId>io.projectreactor</groupId>
  <artifactId>reactor-test</artifactId>
  <scope>test</scope>
</dependency>
<dependency>
  <groupId>org.springframework.boot</groupId>
  <artifactId>spring-boot-starter-test</artifactId>
  <scope>test</scope>
</dependency>
```

As you can see, in the preceding code, all of the dependencies can be scoped for testing purposes.

Test class

Create a normal test class, as follows. Use the @Autowired annotation to inject the WebTestClient instance in your test class:

```
@RunWith(SpringRunner.class)
@SpringBootTest(webEnvironment = SpringBootTest.WebEnvironment.RANDOM_PORT)
@FixMethodOrder(MethodSorters.NAME_ASCENDING)
public class WebclientDemoApplicationTests {
  @Autowired
  private WebTestClient webTestClient;
  @Test
```

```
public void getAllMovies() {
    System.out.println("Test 1 executing getAllMovies");
    webTestClient.get().uri("/api/movie")
            .accept(MediaType.APPLICATION_JSON)
            .exchange()
            .expectStatus().isOk()
            .expectHeader().contentType(MediaType.APPLICATION_JSON)
            .expectBodyList(Movie.class);
}
@Test
public void saveMovie() {
    System.out.println("Test 2 executing saveMovie");
    Movie movie = new Movie(Long.valueOf(10), "Test Title", "Test
Genre");
    webTestClient.post().uri("/api/movie")
            .body(Mono.just(movie), Movie.class)
            .exchange()
            .expectStatus().isOk()
            .expectBody();
}
}
```

The WebTestClient object's functionality is similar to WebClient, as seen earlier. We can check for various properties in the response to ascertain what we want to test. In the preceding example, for the first test, we are firing a GET request and checking for OK status, an application/JSON content type header, and, finally, a body having a list of Movie objects. In the second test, we are firing a POST request with a Movie object as the body, and, expecting an OK status and an empty body.

Spring Data

Even though this book is focused on Spring Security on reactive concepts, I really want you to have some idea of reactive concepts in other areas as well. So, there is a separate project, spring-boot-security-mongo-webflux, which looks at implementing reactive concepts by integrating the earlier project with reactive MongoDB, using Spring Data. Covering every aspect in regard to this is not something that we will do. However, with the earlier project as a base, we will cover some of the important aspects in this section.

Maven dependency

In your application `pom.xml`, add the following dependencies, both dealing with MongoDB inclusion into the project:

```
<!--Mongo-->
<dependency>
    <groupId>org.springframework.boot</groupId>
    <artifactId>spring-boot-starter-data-mongodb-reactive</artifactId>
</dependency>
<dependency>
    <groupId>de.flapdoodle.embed</groupId>
    <artifactId>de.flapdoodle.embed.mongo</artifactId>
    <scope>test</scope>
</dependency>
```

I have installed MongoDB on my machine. I have started the database locally on the default port (`27017`).

MongoDB configuration

Add the following to your application.properties file:

spring.data.mongodb.uri=mongodb://localhost:27017/movie

We will be pointing our DB to a locally running DB on the default port utilizing the movie database.

Setting up a model

In our already existing `Movie` model, we just added one more annotation: `@Document(collection = "movies")`. This annotation will inform MongoDB as to the name of the collection in the DB where this model will be stored.

Implementing a repository

We will create a new repository, `ReactiveMovieRepository`, with our two curated methods and all of the default methods provided by our extended class:

```
@Repository
public interface ReactiveMovieRepository extends
    ReactiveMongoRepository<Movie, Long> {
        @Query("{ 'title': ?0, 'genre': ?1}")
```

```
      Flux<Movie> findByTitleAndGenre(String title, String genre);
      @Query("{ 'genre': ?0}")
      Flux<Movie> findByGenre(String genre);
  }
```

We will extend our repository from `ReactiveMongoRepository`.
`ReactiveMongoRepository` has loads of common methods that can be used right away,
without any trouble. The methods that we have implemented use plain queries against the
MongoDB and return the list.

Implementing a controller

To make it separate from our existing functional-based programming, we have created a
new controller that will expose some of the methods in a RESTful way, using the newly
created `ReactiveMovieRepository`:

```
@RestController
public class MovieController {
  @Autowired
  private ReactiveMovieRepository reactiveMovieRepository;
  @GetMapping("/movies")
  public Flux<Movie> getAllMovies() {
      return reactiveMovieRepository.findAll();
  }
  @GetMapping("/movies/{genre}")
  public Flux<Movie> getAllMoviesByGenre(@PathVariable String genre) {
      return reactiveMovieRepository.findByGenre(genre);
  }
  @GetMapping("/movies/{title}/{genre}")
  public Flux<Movie> getAllMoviesByTitleAndGenre
    (@PathVariable String title, @PathVariable String genre) {
      return reactiveMovieRepository.findByTitleAndGenre(title, genre);
  }
  @PostMapping("/movies")
  public Mono<Movie> createMovies(@Valid @RequestBody Movie movie) {
      return reactiveMovieRepository.save(movie);
  }
}
```

The class is quite straightforward; each method has appropriate mapping and uses
corresponding repository classes to actually do the job.

Running the application

Using the `mongod` command, we will start the locally installed MongoDB and then using the following command, we will start the project we just created:

```
mvn spring-boot:run
```

Head over to postman and call the URL `http://localhost:8080/movies` (GET). You will see an array with zero elements in it. Now, call the URL `http://localhost:8080/movies` (POST), with the following JSON in the body:

```json
{
    "id": 1,
    "title": "testtitle",
    "genre": "thriller"
}
```

You will get a 200 OK status, and should see the newly created JSON as a response. Now, if you run the GET request on movies endpoint, you should see the newly created `Movie` as a response.

Here, we implemented CRUD in our `Movie` model by using MongoDB as a persistence store in a reactive programming paradigm.

Authorization

In the past, we already saw that using the `@EnableWebFluxSecurity` annotation, we can get URL security. Spring Security also allows you to secure method execution in a reactive way, by using another annotation, `@EnableReactiveMethodSecurity`. The concept is the same what we saw in earlier examples based on Spring MVC. We will just cover method security in this section; the rest of the aspects are exactly the same and we will avoid replication here.

Method security

To enable method security, first, annotate the Spring Security configurations class with `@EnableReactiveMethodSecurity`:

```
@EnableReactiveMethodSecurity
public class SpringSecurityWebFluxConfig {
    ...
}
```

After that, for any method that you would like to have some security features for, use all of the various security-related annotations discussed in previous chapters:

```
@GetMapping("/movies")
@PreAuthorize("hasRole('ADMIN')")
public Flux<Movie> getAllMovies() {
  return reactiveMovieRepository.findAll();
}
```

In the preceding method, we are directing Spring Security that the method execution for `getAllMovies()` should be allowed if the user is authenticated and has the `ADMIN` role granted.

Customization

Spring Security allows for a number of customizations. The default pages produced by Spring Security, such as login form, logout form, and so on, can be fully customized in all aspects suiting your application's brand. If you would like to tweak Spring Security's default execution, implementing your own filter is appropriate. Since Spring Security depends heavily on filters to achieve its functionality, let's look at the customization opportunity in this.

In addition, almost all parts of Spring Security can be customized by using your own classes, and then plugged into the Spring Security default flow to manage your own customizations.

Writing custom filters

As we saw earlier, in a WebFlux web application, Spring Security works based on `WebFilter` (similar to Servlet Filter in Spring MVC). If you would like to customize certain aspects in Spring Security, especially in request and response manipulation, implementing a custom `WebFilter` is one of the approaches that can be looked at.

Spring WebFlux offers two approaches to implement filters:

- **Using** `WebFilter`: Works for both annotation-based and functional-based (`routerhandler`)
- **Using** `HandlerFilterFunction`: Works only with functional-based

Using WebFilter

We will be building on top of our project, spring-boot-webflux. To make it isolated from other projects, we will create a new project, spring-boot-webflux-custom. As indicated previously, using WebFilter applies to both annotation-based and functional-based WebFlux approaches. In our example, we'll have two paths: filtertest1 and filtertest2. We will write test cases using WebFluxTestClient, and will assert certain conditions. Being separate from the rest, we will create a new routing config, a handler, and an entirely new REST controller. We will not go into detail on some of the aspects already covered. In this section, we will just go through the WebFilter code, and also some important aspects of the test cases:

```
@Component
public class SampleWebFilter implements WebFilter {
    @Override
    public Mono<Void> filter(ServerWebExchange serverWebExchange,
            WebFilterChain webFilterChain) {
        serverWebExchange.getResponse().getHeaders().add("filter-added-
header",
            "filter-added-header-value");
        return webFilterChain.filter(serverWebExchange);
    }
}
```

The SampleWebFilter class implements WebFilter, and also implements the filter method. In this class, we will add a new response header, filter-added-header:

```
@Test
public void filtertest1_with_pathVariable_equalTo_value1_apply_WebFilter()
{
    EntityExchangeResult<String> result =
        webTestClient.get().uri("/filtertest1/value1")
        .exchange()
        .expectStatus().isOk()
        .expectBody(String.class)
        .returnResult();
    Assert.assertEquals(result.getResponseBody(), "value1");
    Assert.assertEquals(result.getResponseHeaders()
        .getFirst("filter-added-header"), "filter-added-header-value");
}
@Test
public void filtertest2_with_pathVariable_equalTo_value1_apply_WebFilter()
{
    EntityExchangeResult<String> result =
        webTestClient.get().uri("/filtertest2/value1")
        .exchange()
```

```
        .expectStatus().isOk()
        .expectBody(String.class)
        .returnResult();
    Assert.assertEquals(result.getResponseBody(), "value1");
    Assert.assertEquals(result.getResponseHeaders()
        .getFirst("filter-added-header"), "filter-added-header-value");
}
```

In both test cases, for both paths, we will check for newly added headers. When you run the test cases (using `mvn test`), it will confirm this finding.

Using HandlerFilterFunction

We will implement a new `HandlerFilterFunction`, `SampleHandlerFilterFunction`, in which we will look at a path variable (`pathVariable`) and check for its value. If the value is equal to `value2`, we will mark the status as `BAD_REQUEST`. It's important to note that since `HandlerFilterFunction` applies only to functional-based, even though the path variable value is equal to `value2`, the status is not stamped as `BAD_REQUEST`, and the response received is OK:

```
public class SampleHandlerFilterFunction implements
        HandlerFilterFunction<ServerResponse, ServerResponse> {
    @Override
    public Mono<ServerResponse> filter(ServerRequest serverRequest,
        HandlerFunction<ServerResponse> handlerFunction) {
        if (serverRequest.pathVariable("pathVariable")
                .equalsIgnoreCase("value2")) {
            return ServerResponse.status(BAD_REQUEST).build();
        }
        return handlerFunction.handle(serverRequest);
    }
}
```

`SampleHandlerFilterFunction` implements the `HandlerFilterFunction` class, and also implements the `filter` method. In this class, we will explicitly set the response status as a bad request, if a condition is met:

```
@Test
public void
filtertest1_with_pathVariable_equalTo_value2_apply_HandlerFilterFunction()
{
    webTestClient.get().uri("/filtertest1/value2")
        .exchange()
        .expectStatus().isOk();
```

```
}
@Test
public void
filtertest2_with_pathVariable_equalTo_value2_apply_HandlerFilterFunction()
{
    webTestClient.get().uri("/filtertest2/value2")
        .exchange()
        .expectStatus().isBadRequest();
}
```

In the preceding test cases, the path tested is different, and since `HandlerFilterFunction` applies only to functional-based, the response is OK when the path is `filtertest1`, and it's `BAD_REQUEST` when the path is `filtertest2`.

Summary

In this chapter, for the first time in this book, we went over the details of reactive programming, using the Spring WebFlux framework. We started off by giving adequate details on the framework itself at a high level. We went over a very basic example, and then, introduced you to Spring Security and its functionality with Spring WebFlux.

Finally, we went through a hands-on coding session, with a sample application. In this example, we covered other reactive aspects, such as Spring Data Mongo, so as to give you more insight into the reactive world.

We ended the chapter with some of the customization possible in Spring WebFlux with Spring Security.

Having read this chapter, you should have a clear idea of the differences between the Spring MVC and Spring WebFlux frameworks. You should also have a good understanding of the workings of Spring WebFlux security using the Spring Security module. The examples are meant to be simple in nature and as we are undressing Spring Security in this book, those aspects are given more value in the explanations.

REST API Security

6

Spring Security can be used to secure REST APIs. This chapter begins with the introduction of some of the important concepts in regard to REST and the JWT.

The chapter then introduces OAuth concepts and by using hands-on coding examples, explains simple and advanced REST API security utilizing the Spring Security and Spring Boot modules in the Spring Framework.

We will be using the OAuth protocol in our examples to secure exposed REST API's utilizing Spring Security features to the fullest. We will be using the JWT to exchange claims between the server and client.

In this chapter, we will cover the following concepts:

- Modern application architecture
- Reactive REST API
- Simple REST API security
- Advanced REST API security
- Spring Security OAuth project
- OAuth2 and Spring WebFlux
- Spring Boot and OAuth2

Important concepts

Before getting into coding, we need to be conversant with some important concepts. This section is aimed at introducing you to some of these concepts in detail.

REST

Representational State Transfer (**REST**) is an architectural style presented by Roy Fielding in the year 2000 for developing web services. It is built on top of the well-known **Hypertext Transfer Protocol** (**HTTP**) and can transfer data in multiple formats, the most common being **JavaScript Object Notation** (**JSON**) and **eXtensible Markup Language** (**XML**). The status of a request in REST is indicated using standard HTTP status code (200: OK, 404: Page not found!, and so on). Being based on HTTP, security is taken care of using the already familiar **Secure Sockets Layer** (**SSL**) and **Transport Layer Security** (**TLS**).

While writing such web services, you are free to use any programming language (Java, .NET, and so on) that is capable of making web requests based on HTTP (which is a de facto standard that every language supports). You have a number of well-known frameworks, using which developing RESTful APIs on the server side is quite easy and simple. Also, on the client side, there are a number of frameworks that make invoking RESTful APIs and handling responses straightforward and easy.

Since REST works on internet protocol, the caching of a web service response can be achieved quite easily by supplying appropriate HTTP headers (Cache-Control, Expires, and so on). The HTTP methods PUT and DELETE are not cacheable in any scenario. The following table summarizes the use of HTTP methods:

HTTP method	Description
GET	Retrieves a resource
POST	Creates a new resource
PUT	Updates an existing resource
DELETE	Deletes an existing resource
PATCH	Makes a partial update to a resource

Table 1: HTTP method usage

A REST API request/response (data sent over the wire) can be compressed by specifying appropriate HTTP headers, similar to caching. The HTTP header, Accept-Encoding, is sent by the client to the server, to let the server know the compression algorithms it can understand. The server successfully compresses a response and puts out another HTTP header, Content-Encoding, letting the client know which algorithm has to be used to decompress.

JSON Web Token (JWT)

"JSON Web Tokens are an open, industry standard RFC 7519 method for representing claims securely between two parties."

-https://jwt.io/

In the past, the stateless nature of HTTP was circumvented in a web application (most of them are stateful in nature) by associating each request with a session ID created on the server and then stored by the client using cookies. Each request sends the cookie (session ID) in the form of an HTTP header, which gets validated by the server, and a state (a user session) is associated with each request. In modern applications (we will cover this in a bit more detail in the next section), a server-side session ID is replaced with the JWT. The following diagram shows the workings of the JWT:

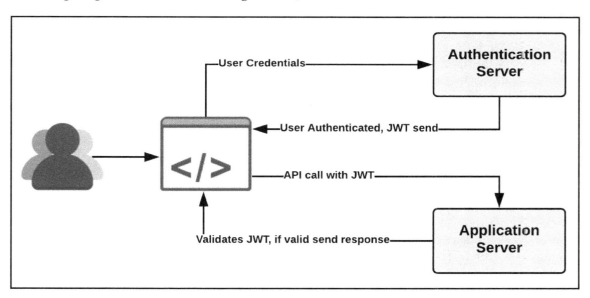

Figure 1: Workings of the JWT in modern applications

The web server, in this case, doesn't create a user session and the user session management capability needed for a stateful application is offloaded to other mechanisms.

In the world of the Spring Framework, the Spring Session module can be employed to externalize the session from the web server to a central persistence store (Redis, Couchbase, and so on). Every request containing a valid token (JWT) is validated against this external store of authenticity and validity. After successful authentication, applications can generate a valid token and send it as a response to the client. The client can then store this token in any client storage mechanism it uses (sessionStorage, localStorage, cookies, and so on, in a browser). Using Spring Security, we can validate this token to ascertain the authenticity and validity of the user and then do whatever is required. We have a dedicated example in a subsequent section (Simple REST API security) of this chapter, which uses a basic authentication mechanism and, if successful, creates the JWT. Subsequent requests use the token in the HTTP header, which gets validated on the server to give access to other secured resources.

The following points highlight some of the advantages of using the JWT:

- **Better performance**: Each request, when reaching the server, has to check the authenticity of the token send. The authenticity of the JWT can be checked locally and doesn't require an external call (say, to a database). This local validation is performant and reduces the overall response time for a request.
- **Simplicity**: JWT is easy and simple to implement. Also, it is a well established format in the industry for tokens. There are a number of well-known libraries which can be used to easily work with the JWT.

Structure of a token

Unlike common security mechanisms, such as encryption, obscuring, and hiding, the JWT doesn't encrypt or hide the data contained within. But, it does the destination system to check whether the token is from an authentic source. The structure of the JWT consists of a header, payload, and a signature. As mentioned, rather than encryption, the data contained within the JWT is encoded and then signed. Encoding does the job of transforming the data in a way that is acceptable by a variety of parties and signing allows us to check for its authenticity and, in fact, its origin:

```
JWT = header.payload.signature
```

Let's go into more detail about each of the components constituting the token.

Header

This is a JSON object and takes the following format. It gives information on how the signature should be computed:

```
{
  "alg": "HS256",
  "typ": "JWT"
}
```

The value of `typ` specifies type of the object, and in this case, it is the `JWT`. The value of `alg` specifies the algorithm used to create the signature, and in this case it is `HMAC-SHA256`.

Payload

The payload forms the actual data (also known as a **claim**) stored in the JWT. According to your application's requirements, you can put any number of claims into your JWT payload component. There are some predefined claims, such as `iss` (issuer), `sub` (subject), `exp` (expiration time), `iat` (issued at), and so on, that can be used, but all of these are optional:

```
{
  "sub": "1234567890",
  "username": "Test User",
  "iat": 1516239022
}
```

Signature

The signature is formed as follows:

1. The `header` is `base64` encoded: `base64(header)`.
2. The `payload` is `base64` encoded: `base64(payload)`.
3. Now join the values in *Step 1* and *Step 2* with a `"."` in the middle:

   ```
   base64UrlEncode(header) + "." +base64UrlEncode(payload)
   ```

4. Now, the signature is attained by hashing, using the algorithm specified in the header, the value attained in *Step 3*, and then appending it with the secret text (say `packtpub`) of your choice:

   ```
   HMACSHA256(
     base64UrlEncode(header) + "." +
     base64UrlEncode(payload),
     packtpub
   )
   ```

The final JWT is as shown here:

```
eyJhbGciOiJIUzI1NiIsInR5cCI6IkpXVCJ9.eyJzdWIiOiIxMjM0NTY3ODkwIiwibmFtZSI6Il
Rlc3QgVXNlciIsImlhdCI6MTUxNjIzOTAyMn0.yzBMVScwv9Ln4vYafpTuaSGa6mUbpwCg84VOh
VTQKBg
```

The website `https://jwt.io/` is a place I always visit for any of my JWT needs. The sample data used in this example is from that site:

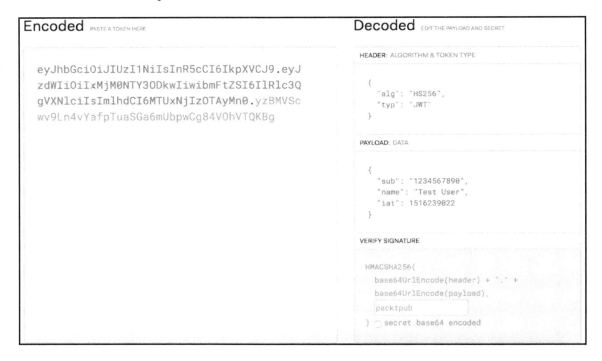

Figure 2: Screen grab from https://jwt.io/

Modern application architecture

Frontends of most modern applications are not built using server-side web application frameworks, such as Spring MVC, **Java Server Faces (JSF)**, and so on. Infact, many are built using full-fledged client-side frameworks, such as React (to be full-fledged, it has to be combined with other libraries), Angular, and so on. The previous statement doesn't mean in any way that there is no place for such server-side web application frameworks. According to the application you are building, there are specific places for each of these frameworks.

When using client-side frameworks, the client code (HTML, JS, CSS, and so on) in general is not secured. However, the data required to render these dynamic pages is secured behind a RESTful endpoint.

To secure a RESTful backend, the JWT is used to exchange claims between the server and the client. The JWT enables the stateless exchange of tokens between the two parties and takes away the burden of session management (no more sticky sessions or session replication between multiple server nodes) by the server. This enables the application to scale horizontally in a cost-effective manner:

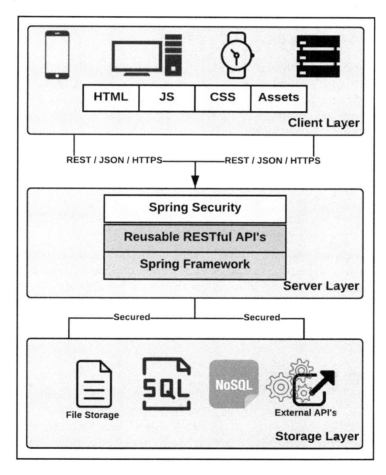

Figure 3: API-based modern application architecture

SOFEA

Service-Oriented Front-End Architecture (**SOFEA**) is of the architectural style which had gained popularity in the past when **Service Oriented Architecture** (**SOA**) and was becoming common in many enterprises. In modern days, SOA is more of less with microservices-based architecture and the backend is reduced to a bunch of RESTful endpoints. The client on the other hand is becoming thicker and uses client-side MVC frameworks such as Angular and React, just to name a couple. However, the core concept of SOFEA, in which backend is just endpoints and frontend (UI) becoming thicker is something everyone considers in modern age web application development.

Some of the advantages of SOFEA are as follows:

- The client in this is thicker (similar to thick client applications) as against thin client web applications that we have seen in the past. After initial view/rendering of pages, all the assets are downloaded from server and resides/caches on the client (browser). Thereafter, the server is contacted only for data when required by the client through XHR (Ajax) calls.
- After the client code is downloaded, only data flows from the server to the client, as opposed to presentation code (HTML, JavaScript, and so on), better utilizing the bandwidth. As there is less data being transferred, response times are faster, making applications perform better.
- Any number of clients can be written utilizing the same RESTful server endpoints, reusing APIs to the fullest.
- These endpoints can externalize a session (in the Spring Framework, there is a module called **Spring Session**, which can be used to achieve this technical capability), thus easily achieving the horizontal scalability of the server.
- Better role segregation of team members in a project with APIs managed by a team and UI code managed by a different team.

Reactive REST API

In the `Chapter 4`, *Authentication Using CAS and JAAS*, we went through the reactive Spring WebFlux web application framework in detail. We also looked into a lot of the reactive programming support provided by the Spring Framework and other Spring modules. Knowingly or unknowingly, we created a reactive REST API in the previous chapter's example sections. We used a handler and router mechanism for creating a RESTful application and also secured it using the *BASIC* authentication mechanism.

We saw the workings of `WebClient` (a reactive way of calling REST APIs, as opposed to using a blocking `RestTemplate`) and `WebTestClient` (a reactive way of writing test cases). We also saw the workings of Spring Data in a reactive way using MongoDB as the persistent store.

We will not go through these aspects here; we will only mention that, if you wish, you can make yourself comfortable with this topic by going through the section in `Chapter 4`, *Authentication Using CAS and JAAS*. In this chapter, we will cover where we left off from the previous chapter by getting to REST API security using the JWT, and then going through REST API security using OAuth (implementing a custom provider as opposed to using public providers, such as Google, Facebook, and so on).

Simple REST API security

We will use the example that we created in `Chapter 5`, *Integrating with Spring WebFlux* (*spring-boot-spring-webflux*) and expand on it by doing the following:

- Bringing the JWT support to the already existing Spring WebFlux application secured using basic authentication.
- Creating a new controller (`path /auth/**`) that will have new endpoints, using which you can authenticate the user.
- Using basic authentication or the auth REST endpoint, we will generate the JWT on the server and send it as a response to the client. Subsequent calls from the client to access secured REST APIs can be achieved by using the JWT supplied as a HTTP header (authorization, bearer token).

We won't be able to go into each and every detail of this project (we have a more important topic that we need to cover in this chapter within the stipulated page count). However, while going through the example, important code snippets will be listed down and explained in detail to some extent.

Spring Security configuration

In the Spring Security configuration, we tweak the `springSecurityFilterChain` bean, as shown in the following code snippet:

```
@Bean
public SecurityWebFilterChain springSecurityFilterChain(ServerHttpSecurity
http){
    AuthenticationWebFilter authenticationJWT = new
```

```
AuthenticationWebFilter(new
UserDetailsRepositoryReactiveAuthenticationManager(userDetailsRepository())
);
    authenticationJWT.setAuthenticationSuccessHandler(new
JWTAuthSuccessHandler());
    http.csrf().disable();
    http
        .authorizeExchange()
        .pathMatchers(WHITELISTED_AUTH_URLS)
        .permitAll()
        .and()
        .addFilterAt(authenticationJWT, SecurityWebFiltersOrder.FIRST)
        .authorizeExchange()
        .pathMatchers(HttpMethod.GET, "/api/movie/**").hasRole("USER")
        .pathMatchers(HttpMethod.POST, "/api/movie/**").hasRole("ADMIN")
        .anyExchange().authenticated()
        .and()
        .addFilterAt(new JWTAuthWebFilter(),
SecurityWebFiltersOrder.HTTP_BASIC);
    return http.build();
}
```

As you can see, we have a new `AuthenticationWebFilter` and a
`AuthenticationSuccessHandler` configured. We also have a new `JWTAuthWebFilter`
class for handling the JWT-based authentication configured.

We will be using `ReactiveUserDetailsService` with hardcoded user credentials for
testing, as shown in the following code snippet:

```
@Bean
public MapReactiveUserDetailsService userDetailsRepository() {
    UserDetails user = User.withUsername("user").password("
        {noop}password").roles("USER").build();
    UserDetails admin = User.withUsername("admin").password("
        {noop}password").roles("USER","ADMIN").build();
    return new MapReactiveUserDetailsService(user, admin);
}
```

Authentication success handler

We set up a custom `AuthenticationSuccessHandler` (the source code for this class is shown next) in our Spring Security configuration class. On successful authentication, it will generate the JWT and also set a HTTP response header:

- **Header name**: `Authorization`
- **Header value**: `Bearer JWT`

Let's take a look at the following code:

```
public class JWTAuthSuccessHandler implements
ServerAuthenticationSuccessHandler{
    @Override
    public Mono<Void> onAuthenticationSuccess(WebFilterExchange
            webFilterExchange, Authentication authentication) {
        ServerWebExchange exchange = webFilterExchange.getExchange();
        exchange.getResponse()
            .getHeaders()
            .add(HttpHeaders.AUTHORIZATION,
                    getHttpAuthHeaderValue(authentication));
        return webFilterExchange.getChain().filter(exchange);
    }
    private static String getHttpAuthHeaderValue(Authentication
authentication){
        return String.join("
","Bearer",tokenFromAuthentication(authentication));
    }
    private static String tokenFromAuthentication(Authentication
authentication){
        return new JWTUtil().generateToken(
            authentication.getName(),
            authentication.getAuthorities());
    }
}
```

The `JWTUtil` class contains a number of utility methods dealing with the JWTs, such as the generation of tokens, verification of tokens, and so on. The `generateToken` method in the `JWTUtil` class is as shown here:

```
public static String generateToken(String subjectName, Collection<? extends
GrantedAuthority> authorities) {
    JWTClaimsSet claimsSet = new JWTClaimsSet.Builder()
        .subject(subjectName)
        .issuer("javacodebook.com")
        .expirationTime(new Date(new Date().getTime() + 30 * 1000))
```

```
        .claim("auths", authorities.parallelStream().map(auth ->
    (GrantedAuthority) auth).map(a ->
            a.getAuthority()).collect(Collectors.joining(",")))
        .build();
    SignedJWT signedJWT = new SignedJWT(new JWSHeader(JWSAlgorithm.HS256),
claimsSet);
    try {
        signedJWT.sign(JWTUtil.getJWTSigner());
    } catch (JOSEException e) {
        e.printStackTrace();
    }
    return signedJWT.serialize();
}
```

Custom WebFilter namely JWTAuthWebFilter

Our custom `WebFilter`, named `JWTAuthWebFilter`, is entrusted with converting the JWT token received into appropriate classes that the Spring Security understands. It makes use of a converter named `JWTAuthConverter`, which does a number of things, as follows:

- Gets the authorization `payload`
- Extracts the token by discarding the `Bearer` string
- Verifies the token
- Creates a `UsernamePasswordAuthenticationToken` class understood by Spring Security

The code snippet below shows the `JWTAuthWebFilter` class and its important method which does operations listed above.

```
public class JWTAuthConverter implements Function<ServerWebExchange,
        Mono<Authentication>> {
    @Override
    public Mono<Authentication> apply(ServerWebExchange serverWebExchange)
{
        return Mono.justOrEmpty(serverWebExchange)
            .map(JWTUtil::getAuthorizationPayload)
            .filter(Objects::nonNull)
            .filter(JWTUtil.matchBearerLength())
            .map(JWTUtil.getBearerValue())
            .filter(token -> !token.isEmpty())
            .map(JWTUtil::verifySignedJWT)
            .map(JWTUtil::getUsernamePasswordAuthenticationToken)
            .filter(Objects::nonNull);
    }
```

```
}
```

After this conversion, it does the actual authentication using Spring Security, which sets `SecurityContext` in the application, as shown in the following code snippet:

```
@Override
public Mono<Void> filter(ServerWebExchange exchange, WebFilterChain chain)
{
    return this.getAuthMatcher().matches(exchange)
        .filter(matchResult -> matchResult.isMatch())
        .flatMap(matchResult -> this.jwtAuthConverter.apply(exchange))
        .switchIfEmpty(chain.filter(exchange).then(Mono.empty()))
        .flatMap(token -> authenticate(exchange, chain, token));
}
//..more methods
private Mono<Void> authenticate(ServerWebExchange exchange,
                                WebFilterChain chain, Authentication token) {
    WebFilterExchange webFilterExchange = new WebFilterExchange(exchange,
chain);
    return this.reactiveAuthManager.authenticate(token)
       .flatMap(authentication -> onAuthSuccess(authentication,
           webFilterExchange));
}
private Mono<Void> onAuthSuccess(Authentication authentication,
WebFilterExchange
        webFilterExchange) {
    ServerWebExchange exchange = webFilterExchange.getExchange();
    SecurityContextImpl securityContext = new SecurityContextImpl();
    securityContext.setAuthentication(authentication);
    return this.securityContextRepository.save(exchange, securityContext)
        .then(this.authSuccessHandler
        .onAuthenticationSuccess(webFilterExchange, authentication))
.subscriberContext(ReactiveSecurityContextHolder.withSecurityContext(
        Mono.just(securityContext)));
}
```

The `JWTAuthWebFilter` class filter method does the necessary conversions and then the `authenticate` method does the actual authentication, and finally calls the `onAuthSuccess` method.

New controller classes

We have two controllers, namely `DefaultController` (mapped to the / and /login paths) and `AuthController` (mapped to the /auth main route and /token sub-route). The /auth/token path can be used to retrieve the token, which can be used for a subsequent API call (`Bearer <Token>`). The code snippet for `AuthController` is as shown here:

```
@RestController
@RequestMapping(path = "/auth", produces = { APPLICATION_JSON_UTF8_VALUE })
public class AuthController {

    @Autowired
    private MapReactiveUserDetailsService userDetailsRepository;
        @RequestMapping(method = POST, value = "/token")
        @CrossOrigin("*")
        public Mono<ResponseEntity<JWTAuthResponse>> token(@RequestBody
                JWTAuthRequest jwtAuthRequest) throws
AuthenticationException {
                String username =  jwtAuthRequest.getUsername();
                String password =  jwtAuthRequest.getPassword();
                return userDetailsRepository.findByUsername(username)
                    .map(user -> ok().contentType(APPLICATION_JSON_UTF8).body(
                        new
JWTAuthResponse(JWTUtil.generateToken(user.getUsername(),
user.getAuthorities()), user.getUsername())))
                        .defaultIfEmpty(notFound().build());
        }
    }
}
```

Running the application and testing

Run the application using the Spring Boot command shown below:

```
mvn spring-boot:run
```

I will be using Postman to execute the REST endpoints.

You can get hold of the token, to include it in subsequent calls, by employing two methods as detailed below:

- If you access any route using basic authentication credentials, in the response header, you should get the token. I will be using the `/login` path with **Basic Auth** (authorization header) to get the token, as shown here:

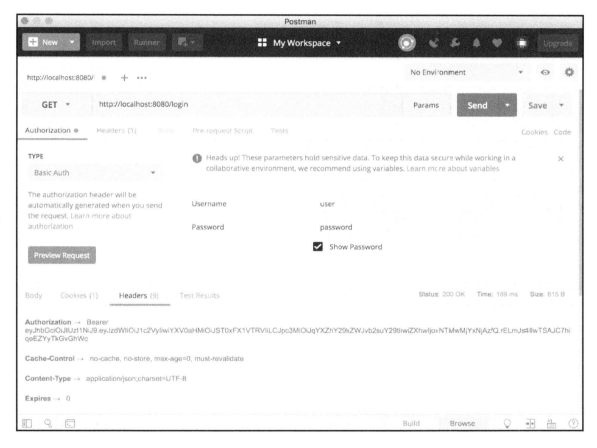

Figure 4: Getting token using Basic Auth in Postman

- Access the `/auth/token` endpoint with **Basic Auth** credentials supplied in the form of JSON (using the `JWTAuthRequest` class), as shown here, in Postman:

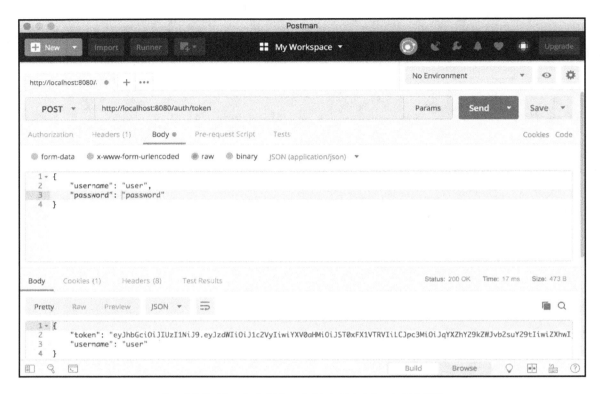

Figure 5: Getting token using /auth/token endpoint using Basic Auth credentials in JSON

Using the token retrieved, call the movie endpoint, as shown here, using Postman:

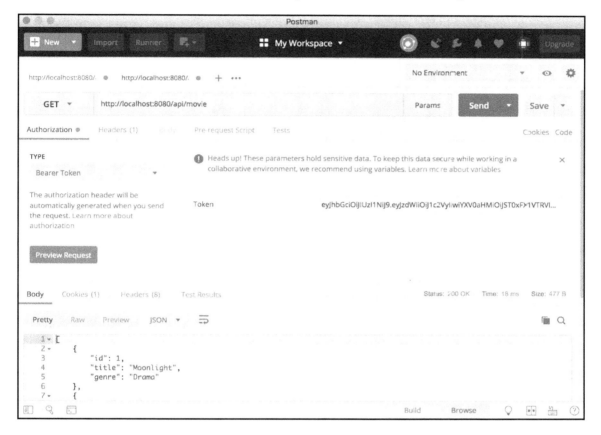

Figure 6: Retrieving movie listing using a JWT token in Postman

This completes the example that we were building. In this example, we secured the REST APIs by making use of JWT and validated them using Spring Security. As mentioned, this is a basic way in which you can secure your REST APIs using Spring Security with JWTs.

Advanced REST API security

REST APIs can be secured by another mechanism in your web application, OAuth.

OAuth is an authorization framework that allows other applications with the right credentials access to partial/limited user profile details stored on platforms such as Google and Facebook. The authentication part is delegated to these services and if successful, appropriate grants are given to the calling client/application, which can be used to get access to secured resources (in our case RESTful APIs).

We have seen OAuth security using a public authentication provider in Chapter 3, *Authentication Using CAS and JAAS* (in the *OAuth 2 and OpenID connect* section). However, we need not use these public providers; you have the choice of using your own. We will cover one such example in this chapter, where we will be using our own authentication provider and securing our Spring Boot-based reactive REST endpoints.

Before getting into the example, we need to understand a bit more about OAuth, and also need to understand its various components. We already went through a lot of the details of OAuth in Chapter 3, *Authentication Using CAS and JAAS*. We will add to those details in this section and then go through the code example.

OAuth2 roles

OAuth stipulates four roles for users and applications. The interactions between these roles are shown in the following diagram:

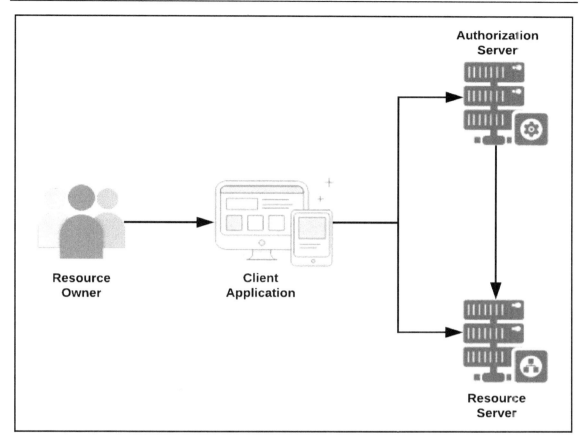

Figure 7: OAuth role interaction

We will look into each of these OAuth roles in some detail.

Resource owner

This is the user who owns the protected resource that is needed by the consuming client application. If we take Facebook or Google as the authentication provider, the resource owner is the actual user who has data saved on these platforms.

Resource server

This is the server that has the secured resources in the form of hosted APIs. If we take Google or Facebook as an example, they hold the profile information, as well as other information, in the form of APIs. If the client application successfully authenticates (using the credentials provided by the user) and then the user grants appropriate permissions, they can get access to this information through their exposed APIs.

Client

This is the application that to access the secured resources available on the resource server. If the user is successfully authenticated and the client application is given permission by the user to access the right information, the client application can retrieve the data.

Authorization server

This is the server that authenticates and authorizes client applications to access the secured resources owned by the resource owner and on the resource server. It is not uncommon to see the same server performing both roles.

To participate in OAuth, your application has to first register with the service provider (Google , Facebook, and so on) against which you plan to authenticate by providing the application name, application URL, and callback URL. Successful registration of your application with the service provider gives you two values unique to your application: `client application_id` and `client_secret`. `client_id` can be exposed publicly but `client_secret` is kept hidden (private). Both these values are needed whenever you access the service provider. The following diagram shows the interactions between these roles:

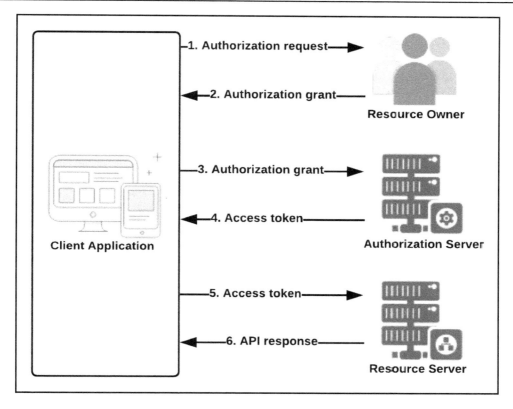

Figure 8: OAuth role interaction

The steps in the preceding diagram are covered in detail here:

1. The client application requests the resource owner to give them authorization to access the secured resources
2. If the resource owner authorizes this, the authorization grant is sent to the client application
3. The client application asks for a token, using the grant provided by the resource owner along with authentication credentials from the authorization server
4. If the credentials and grant from the client application are valid, the authorization server issues an Access Token to the client application
5. The client application accesses the protected resources on the resource server using the Access Token provided
6. If the Access Token sent by the client application is valid, the resource server gives access to the secured resources

Authorization grant types

As shown in the diagram, for the client to start calling APIs, it needs to obtain an authorization grant in the form of an Access Token. OAuth provides four grant types, which can be used according to different application requirements. The as to which authorization grant type to use is left with the client application.

Authorization code flow

This a is very commonly used grant type and works on redirection at the server. It is highly suitable for server-side applications where the source code is hosted on the server and nothing is available on the client. The following diagram explains the authorization code grant type flow:

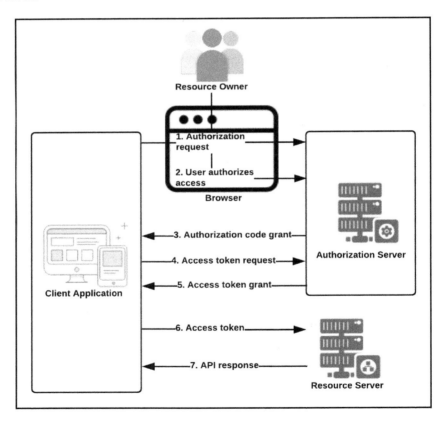

Figure 9: Authorization code flow

The steps in the preceding diagram are explained in detail here:

1. The resource owner of the secured resource is presented with a screen in the browser to authorize the request. Here is a sample authorization link: `https://<DOMAIN>/oauth/authorize?response_type=code&client_id=< CLIENT_ID>&redirect_uri=<CALLBACK_URL>&scope=<SCOPE>`.

   These are the important query parameters in the previous link:

   - `client_id`: The client application ID that we got while registering the application with the service provider
   - `redirect_uri`: After successful authorization, the server redirects to this URL supplied
   - `response_type`: A very important parameter the client uses to ask the server for the authorization code
   - `scope`: Specifies the level of access that it requires

2. If the resource owner (user) allows this, they click on the authorize link, which is sent to the authorization server.

3. If the authorization request sent to the authorization server is validated and found to be successful, the client receives the authorization code grant from the authorization server appended as a query parameter in the callback URL (`<CALLBACK_URL>?code=<AUTHORIZATION_CODE>`) specified in `Step 1`.

4. Using the authorization grant, the client application requests an Access Token from the authorization server (`https://<DOMAIN>/oauth/token?client_id=<CLIENT_ID>&client_secr et=<CLIENT_SECRET>&grant_type=authorization_code&code=<AUTHORIZ ATION_CODE>&redirect_uri=CALLBACK_URL`).

   In this URL, the client application's `client_secret` also has to be passed, along with the `grant_type` parameter, which states that the code passed is the authorization code.

5. The authorization server validates the credentials and authorization grant and sends the Access Token to the client application, preferably in the form of JSON.

6. The client application calls the protected resource on the resource server using the Access Token received in *Step 5*.

7. If the Access Token supplied in *Step 5* is valid, the resource server gives access to the secured resource.

Implicit flow

This is commonly used in mobile and web applications, and also works based on redirection. The following diagram explains the implicit code grant type flow:

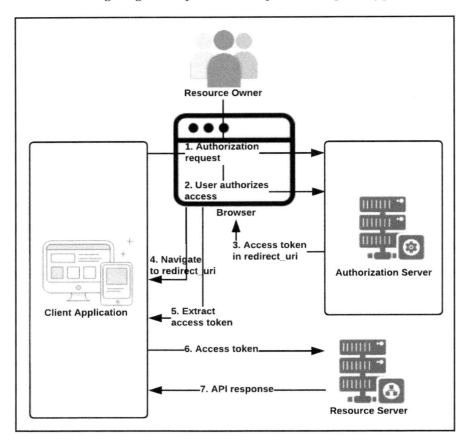

Figure 10: Implicit flow

The steps in the preceding diagram are explained in detail here:

1. The resource owner is presented with a screen (browser) to authorize the request. Here is an example authorization link:
   ```
   https://<DOMAIN>/oauth/authorize?response_type=token&client_id=
   CLIENT_ID&redirect_uri=CALLBACK_URL&scope=<SCOPE>.
   ```

It is important to note that the `response_type` specified in the previous link is `token`. This indicates the server should give the Access Token (this is one of the main differences from the authorization code flow grant type discussed in the previous section).

2. If the resource owner (user) allows this, they click on the authorize link, which is sent to the authorization server.

3. The user-agent (browser or mobile app) receives the Access Token in the `CALLBACK_URL`
   specified (`https://<CALLBACK_URL>#token=<ACCESS_TOKEN>`).

4. The user-agent goes to the specified `CALLBACK_URL`, retaining the Access Token.

5. The client application opens the web page (using any mechanism), which extracts the Access Token from the `CALLBACK_URL`.

6. The client application now has access to the Access Token.

7. The client application calls the secured API using the Access Token.

Client credentials

This is one the simplest grant to implement. The client application sends credentials (the client's service account), along with `client_ID` and `client_secret`, to the authorization server. If the supplied values are valid, the authorization server sends the Access Token, which can be used to get access to the secured resources.

Resource owner password credentials

Again, this is another simple type that can be easily used, but it is considered the most insecure of all. In this grant type, the resource owner (user) has to key their credentials directly into the client application interface (remember, the client application has access to the resource owner's credentials). The credentials are then used by the client application to send to the authorization server to get the Access Token. This grant type only works if the resource owner fully trusts the application through which they give their credentials to the service provider, as these credentials pass through the application server of the client application (they can therefore be stored, if the client application decides to).

Access Token and Refresh Token

The Access Token can be used by the client application to retrieve information from the resource server for a stipulated time for which the token is deemed valid. After this, the server will reject the request with the appropriate HTTP response error code.

Along with the Access Token, OAuth allows the authorization server to also send another token, the Refresh Token. When the Access Token expires, the client application can use this second token to request the authorization server to provide a new Access Token.

Spring Security OAuth project

Currently in the Spring ecosystem, OAuth support has spread to a number of projects, including Spring Security Cloud, Spring Security OAuth, Spring Boot, and the edition of Spring Security (5.x+). This has created a lot of confusion within the community and no single source of ownership. The approach taken by the Spring team is to consolidate this and start maintaining everything regarding to OAuth with Spring Security. Important components that are part of OAuth, namely the authorization server, the resource server, and next-level support for OAuth2, as well as OpenID Connect 1.0, are expected to be added to Spring Security by the end of 2018. The Spring Security roadmap clearly states that by mid-2018, support for the resource server would be added, and the authorization server by the end of 2018.

The Spring Security OAuth project, as it stands at the time of writing this book, is in maintenance mode. This means that there will be a release for bug/security fixes, along with minor features. No major features are planned to be added to this project going forward.

The full OAuth2 feature matrix available in various Spring projects can be found at `https://github.com/spring-projects/spring-security/wiki/OAuth-2.0-Features-Matrix`.

At the time of writing this book, most of the features that we require to implement OAuth is available as part Spring Security OAuth project, which is in maintenance mode.

OAuth2 and Spring WebFlux

Full-fledged OAuth2 support for a Spring WebFlux application is not available in Spring Security at the time of writing this book. However, there is a community urgency around this and many things are slowly and steadily getting into Spring Security in this regard. Many examples are also getting baked into the Spring Security project that show OAuth2 with Spring WebFlux. In the Chapter 5, *Integrating with Spring WebFlux*, we saw one such example in detail. As of writing this book, Spring Security OAuth2 has a hard dependency on Spring MVC.

Spring Boot and OAuth2

As of writing this book, Spring Boot has announced that it is dropping support for the Spring Security OAuth module. Instead, it will from now on with the Spring Security 5.x OAuth2 login features.

A new module named Spring Security OAuth Boot 2 Autoconfig (its dependency in pom.xml is as shown in the following code snippet), ported from Spring Boot 1.5.x, can be used to integrate Spring Security with Spring Boot:

```
<dependency>
  <groupId>org.springframework.security.oauth.boot</groupId>
  <artifactId>spring-security-oauth2-autoconfigure</artifactId>
</dependency>
```

The project source code can be found at https://github.com/spring-projects/spring-security-oauth2-boot). The full documentation for this module can be found at https://docs.spring.io/spring-security-oauth2-boot/docs/current-SNAPSHOT/reference/htmlsingle/.

Sample project

In our sample project, we will set up our own authorization server, against which we will authorize the APIs exposed through our resource server. We have movie APIs exposed on our resource server, and the client application will authenticate with the application (the client application is Spring Security protected) and then try accessing one of the movie APIs, at which point the OAuth flow will kick in. After a successful authorization check with the authorization server, the client will be given access to the requested movie APIs.

We will have a parent project containing three Spring Boot projects: `oauth-authorization-server`, `oauth-resource-server`, and `oauth-client-app`:

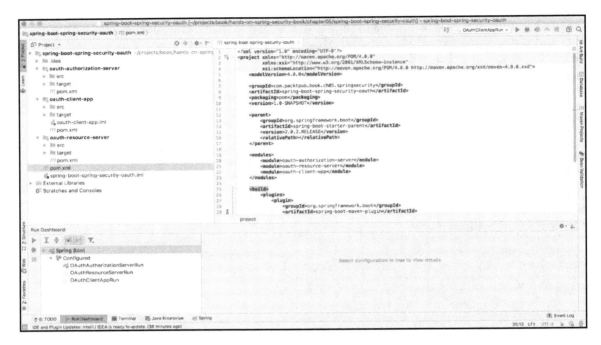

Figure 11: Project structure in IntelliJ

We will now look at each of the individual Spring Boot projects in the subsequent sections. The full source code is available on the book's GitHub page under the `spring-boot-spring-security-oauth` project.

Authorization server

This is a conventional Spring Boot project, which implements the authorization server OAuth role.

Maven dependencies

The main dependencies to be included in the Spring Boot project's `pom.xml` file are as shown in the following code snippet:

```
<!--Spring Boot-->
<dependency>
  <groupId>org.springframework.boot</groupId>
  <artifactId>spring-boot-starter-web</artifactId>
</dependency>
<dependency>
  <groupId>org.springframework.boot</groupId>
  <artifactId>spring-boot-starter-security</artifactId>
</dependency>
<!--OAuth-->
<dependency>
  <groupId>org.springframework.security.oauth</groupId>
  <artifactId>spring-security-oauth2</artifactId>
  <version>2.3.2.RELEASE</version>
</dependency>
<!--JWT-->
<dependency>
  <groupId>org.springframework.security</groupId>
  <artifactId>spring-security-jwt</artifactId>
  <version>1.0.9.RELEASE</version>
</dependency>
```

Spring Boot run class

There is nothing special in this Spring Boot run class, as shown in the following code snippet:

```
@SpringBootApplication
public class OAuthAuthorizationServerRun extends
SpringBootServletInitializer {
  public static void main(String[] args) {
      SpringApplication.run(OAuthAuthorizationServerRun.class, args);
  }
}
```

Spring Security config

The Spring Security config class extends `WebSecurityConfigurerAdapter`. We will override three methods, as shown in the following code snippet:

```
@Configuration
@EnableWebSecurity
public class SpringSecurityConfig extends WebSecurityConfigurerAdapter {
  @Autowired
  private BCryptPasswordEncoder passwordEncoder;
  @Autowired
  public void globalUserDetails(final AuthenticationManagerBuilder auth)
throws
        Exception {
      auth
          .inMemoryAuthentication()
          .withUser("user").password(passwordEncoder.encode("password"))
          .roles("USER")
          .and()
          .withUser("admin").password(passwordEncoder.encode("password"))
          .roles("USER", "ADMIN");
  }
  //...
}
```

We `autowire` the password encoder. We then override the following methods: `globalUserDetails`, `authenticationManagerBean`, and `configure`. There isn't anything special to mention here. We define two users, managed in-memory (user and admin).

Authorization server config

This is the the most important in this Spring Boot project, where we will set up the authorization server configuration. We will use a new annotation, `@EnableAuthorizationServer`. Our configuration class will extend `AuthorizationServerConfigurerAdapter`. We will be using the JWT token store and will also showcase a token enhancer, using which you can enhance your JWT token with more claims, if deemed necessary for your application. The most important method in this configuration class is extracted as the following code snippet:

```
@Override
public void configure(final ClientDetailsServiceConfigurer clients) throws
        Exception {
  clients.inMemory()
      .withClient("oAuthClientAppID")
```

```
        .secret(passwordEncoder().encode("secret"))
        .authorizedGrantTypes("password", "authorization_code",
"refresh_token")
        .scopes("movie", "read", "write")
        .accessTokenValiditySeconds(3600)
        .refreshTokenValiditySeconds(2592000)
        .redirectUris("http://localhost:8080/movie/",
            "http://localhost:8080/movie/index");
}
```

This is where we set up the client-related OAuth configuration. We set up just one client, and we use the in-memory option to make the example simpler to understand. Throughout the application, we will be using BCrypt as our password encoder. The client ID for our client app is oAuthClientAppID and the client secret is secret. We set up three grant types and while accessing the client, we need to specify the necessary scopes (movie, read, and write). After successful execution, the authorization server will redirect you to the specified URL (http://localhost:8080/movie/ or http://localhost:8080/movie/index). If the URL is not correctly specified by the client, the server will throw an error.

The JWT token store and enhancer-related methods are as shown in the following code snippet:

```
@Bean
@Primary
public DefaultTokenServices tokenServices() {
  final DefaultTokenServices defaultTokenServices = new
DefaultTokenServices();
  defaultTokenServices.setTokenStore(tokenStore());
  defaultTokenServices.setSupportRefreshToken(true);
  return defaultTokenServices;
}
@Override
public void configure(final AuthorizationServerEndpointsConfigurer
endpoints)
    throws Exception {
  final TokenEnhancerChain tokenEnhancerChain = new TokenEnhancerChain();
  tokenEnhancerChain.setTokenEnhancers(Arrays.asList(tokenEnhancer(),
    accessTokenConverter()));
  endpoints.tokenStore(tokenStore()).tokenEnhancer(tokenEnhancerChain)
    .authenticationManager(authenticationManager);
}
@Bean
public TokenStore tokenStore() {
  return new JwtTokenStore(accessTokenConverter());
}
```

```
@Bean
public JwtAccessTokenConverter accessTokenConverter() {
  final JwtAccessTokenConverter converter = new JwtAccessTokenConverter();
  converter.setSigningKey("secret");
  return converter;
}
@Bean
public TokenEnhancer tokenEnhancer() {
  return new CustomTokenEnhancer();
}
```

In this code, we specify the token store, which will be used in the `tokenStore` method, and we also declare a `tokenEnhancer` bean. To showcase the token enhancer, we will be using a custom class named `CustomTokenEnhancer`; the class is as shown in the following code snippet:

```
public class CustomTokenEnhancer implements TokenEnhancer {
  @Override
  public OAuth2AccessToken enhance(OAuth2AccessToken accessToken,
    OAuth2Authentication authentication) {
      final Map<String, Object> additionalInfo = new HashMap<>();
      additionalInfo.put("principalinfo",
        authentication.getPrincipal().toString());
      ((DefaultOAuth2AccessToken)accessToken)
        .setAdditionalInformation(additionalInfo);
      return accessToken;
  }
}
```

The custom token `enhancer` class implements `TokenEnhancer`. We just add new information (`principalinfo`) into the JWT token that contains the `toString` version of the `principal` object.

Application properties

Since we are running all three servers locally, we have to specify different ports. Also, it's important that the authorization server runs on a different context path. The following code snippet shows what we have in our `application.properties` file:

```
server.servlet.context-path=/oauth-server
server.port=8082
```

Being a Spring Boot project, it can be run by executing the `mvn spring-boot:run` command.

Resource server

This is a conventional Spring Boot project, which implements the resource server OAuth role.

Maven dependencies

There isn't anything new that we are going to add in our `pom.xml`. The same dependencies that we had in our authorization server project apply here.

Spring Boot run class

This is a typical Spring Boot run class, into which we put the `@SpringBootApplication` annotation, which does all the magic behind the scenes. Again, nothing specific in our Spring Boot run class applies to this project.

Resource server config

This is the main resource server configuration class, where we annotate it with the `@EnableResourceServer` annotation and extend it from `ResourceServerConfigurerAdapter`, as shown in the following code snippet:

```
@Configuration
@EnableResourceServer
public class ResourceServerConfig extends ResourceServerConfigurerAdapter {
  @Autowired
  private CustomAccessTokenConverter customAccessTokenConverter;
  @Override
  public void configure(final HttpSecurity http) throws Exception {
     http.sessionManagement()
        .sessionCreationPolicy(SessionCreationPolicy.ALWAY)
        .and()
        .authorizeRequests().anyRequest().permitAll();
  }
  @Override
  public void configure(final ResourceServerSecurityConfigurer config) {
     config.tokenServices(tokenServices());
  }
```

```
@Bean
public TokenStore tokenStore() {
    return new JwtTokenStore(accessTokenConverter());
}
@Bean
public JwtAccessTokenConverter accessTokenConverter() {
    final JwtAccessTokenConverter converter = new
JwtAccessTokenConverter();
    converter.setAccessTokenConverter(customAccessTokenConverter);
    converter.setSigningKey("secret");
    converter.setVerifierKey("secret");
    return converter;
}
@Bean
@Primary
public DefaultTokenServices tokenServices() {
    final DefaultTokenServices defaultTokenServices =
      new DefaultTokenServices();
    defaultTokenServices.setTokenStore(tokenStore());
    return defaultTokenServices;
}
}
```

Spring Security config

Being the resource server, we are enabling global method security so that every method
exposing an API is secured, as shown in the following code snippet:

```
@Configuration
@EnableGlobalMethodSecurity(prePostEnabled = true)
public class SpringSecurityConfig extends GlobalMethodSecurityConfiguration
{
  @Override
  protected MethodSecurityExpressionHandler createExpressionHandler() {
      return new OAuth2MethodSecurityExpressionHandler();
  }
}
```

Here, we are using `OAuth2MethodSecurityExpressionHandler` as the method security
exception handler so that we can use annotations, as follows:

```
@PreAuthorize("#oauth2.hasScope('movie') and #oauth2.hasScope('read')")
```

Spring MVC config class

We have seen Spring MVC configuration in detail in previous chapters. In our example, it's a very basic Spring MVC `config` class in which `@EnableWebMvc` is used and implements `WebMvcConfigurer`.

Controller class

We have one controller class, which exposes just one method (we can extend it further to expose more APIs). This method lists all the movies in the hardcoded movie list under a URL, `/movie`, as shown in the following code snippet:

```
@RestController
public class MovieController {
    @RequestMapping(value = "/movie", method = RequestMethod.GET)
    @ResponseBody
    @PreAuthorize("#oauth2.hasScope('movie') and #oauth2.hasScope('read')")
    public Movie[] getMovies() {
        initIt();//Movie list initialization
        return movies;
    }
    //...
}
```

We are using a `Movie` model class utilizing all the features of the `lombok` library, as shown in the following code snippet:

```
@Data
@ToString
@Builder
@NoArgsConstructor
@AllArgsConstructor
public class Movie {
  private Long id;
  private String title;
  private String genre;
}
```

It has three attributes and the annotations will do all the magic and keep the model concise.

Application properties

Similar to the authorization server, `application.properties` just has the context path and port assigned.

Being a Spring Boot project, it can be run by executing the `mvn spring-boot:run` command.

Client application

This is a conventional Spring Boot project, which implements the client OAuth role.

Maven dependencies

In our Spring Boot `pom.xml` file, new Maven dependencies for `Thymeleaf` and for the `lombok` library are added. The rest are all typical of a Spring Boot `pom.xml` file, which you are now conversant with.

Spring Boot class

In our example Spring Boot `run` class, there isn't anything worth mentioning. It is a simple class containing the all-important `main` method and the `@SpringBootApplication` annotation.

OAuth client config

This is the main configuration class in the client application, which is annotated with `@EnableOAuth2Client`, as shown in the following code snippet:

```
@Configuration
@EnableOAuth2Client
public class OAuthClientConfig {
  @Autowired
  private OAuth2ClientContext oauth2ClientContext;

  @Autowired
  @Qualifier("movieAppClientDetails")
  private OAuth2ProtectedResourceDetails movieAppClientDetails;

  @ConfigurationProperties(prefix = "security.oauth2.client.movie-app-
client")
  @Bean
  public OAuth2ProtectedResourceDetails movieAppClientDetails() {
      return new AuthorizationCodeResourceDetails();
  }
  @Bean
```

```
public BCryptPasswordEncoder passwordEncoder() {
    return new BCryptPasswordEncoder();
}
@Bean
public OAuth2RestTemplate movieAppRestTemplate() {
    return new OAuth2RestTemplate(movieAppClientDetails,
oauth2ClientContext);
}
}
```

The important aspect to look at in this class is that we initialize the OAuth2 REST template by providing the client details, which are configured in the `application.yml` file.

Spring Security config

In the Spring Security `config` class, we set up the user credentials (in-memory) that can be used to log in to the application and can access secured resources. In the `configure` method, some of the resources are marked as secured and some as unsecured.

Controller classes

We have two controller classes, `SecuredController` and `NonSecuredController`. As the name suggests, one is for declared secured routes and the other for unsecured routes. The `main` method in the secured controller that we are interested is shown in the following code snippet:

```
@RequestMapping(value = "/movie/index", method = RequestMethod.GET)
@ResponseBody
public Movie[] index() {
  Movie[] movies = movieAppRestTemplate
    .getForObject(movieApiBaseUri, Movie[].class);
  return movies;
}
```

We copied the `model` class used in the resource server project into the client application project as well. In an ideal scenario, all this common stuff would be converted into reusable JARs and set up as a dependency to both the projects.

Templates

The templates are quite straightforward. The root context of the application redirects the user to an unsecured page. We have our own custom login page and after a successful login, the user is navigated to a secured page containing a link to the secured OAuth-backed movie listing API.

Application properties

In this project, we are using `application.yml` files and the code is as follows:

```
server:
  port: 8080
spring:
  thymeleaf:
    cache: false
security:
  oauth2:
    client:
      movie-app-client:
        client-id: oAuthClientAppID
        client-secret: secret
        user-authorization-uri:
http://localhost:8082/oauth-server/oauth/authorize
        access-token-uri: http://localhost:8082/oauth-server/oauth/token
        scope: read, write, movie
        pre-established-redirect-uri: http://localhost:8080/movie/index
movie:
  base-uri: http://localhost:8081/oauth-resource/movie
```

The very important aspect of this YML file is the `movie-app-client` properties setup. Again, being a Spring Boot project, it can be run by executing the `mvn spring-boot:run` command.

Running the project

Start all the projects individually using the Spring Boot `mvn spring-boot:run` command. I am using Spring Dashboard in IntelliJ, where I can launch all the projects, as shown in the following screenshot:

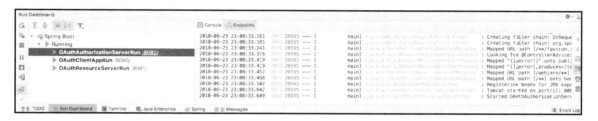

Figure 12: Spring Dashboard in IntelliJ

Navigate to `http://localhost:8080` and you will be redirected to the unsecured page of the client application, as shown here:

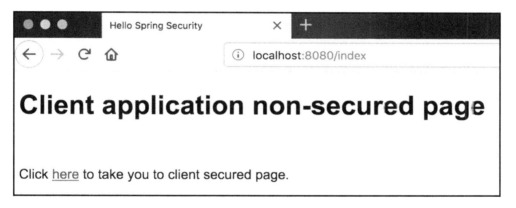

Figure 13: Unsecured page of client app

Click on the link, and you will be taken to the custom login page, as shown here:

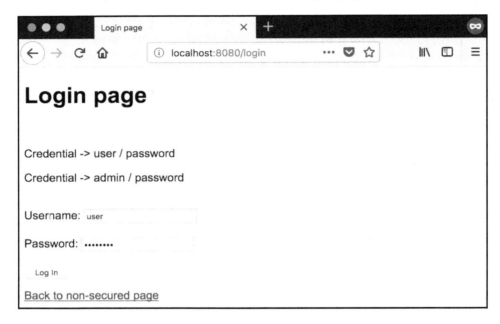

Figure 14: Custom login page of client app

Enter the username/password as required on the page; then, clicking on **Log In** will take you to the secured page, as shown here:

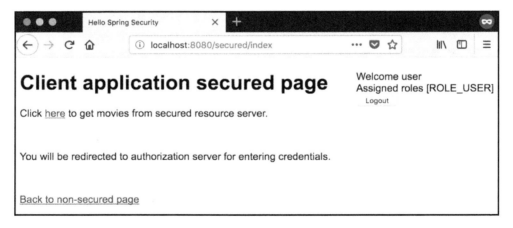

Figure 15: Secured page in client app

Click on the movie API link, and you will be taken to the OAuth flow and then to the authorization server default login page to enter credentials, as shown here:

Figure 16: Authorization server login page

Enter the username/password (we have kept that as user/password) and click on the **Login** button. You will be taken to the authorization page, as shown in the following screenshot:

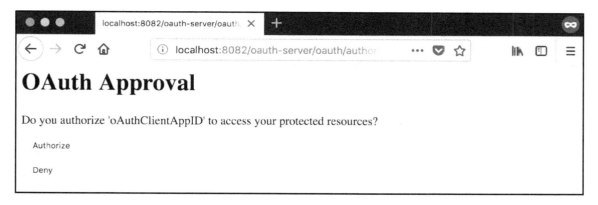

Figure 17: Authorization page on authorization server

Click on **Authorize** and you will be taken back to the client application page, which displays all the movies from the resource server, as shown here:

Figure 18: Movie listing page in the client app displaying a movie API exposed on resource server

With this, we have completed our sample application, in which we have implemented all the roles that are part of OAuth.

Summary

We started this chapter by introducing you to some of the important concepts that are needed to follow along with it. We then covered the important characteristics needed in a modern web application. We quickly covered an architecture called **SOFEA**, which aptly covers how we would like to build modern applications. We then got our hands dirty by implementing security for REST APIs in the simplest of ways.

In the following section, we covered how we can secure a REST API in a more advanced fashion employing OAuth, using a JWT. We started this section by introducing many concepts in regards to OAuth and finally concluded the chapter with a full-fledged sample project that uses OAuth and JWT.

After reading this chapter, you should have a clear understanding of REST, OAuth, and JWT. You should also be comfortable with using Spring Security in the next chapter, to secure the RESTful endpoints exposed in your application.

Spring Security Add-Ons

In previous chapters, we covered the implementation details of the multiple ways in which core security aspects, such as authentication and authorization, use Spring Security. In doing so, we just skimmed over a very thin layer of the capabilities that can be achieved using Spring Security. In this chapter, we will cover some other capabilities provided by Spring Security in a concise manner.

In addition, the chapter introduces many products (open source and paid versions) that can be considered for use along with Spring Security. I am not backing any of these products, but I do consider them strong contenders for achieving the technical capabilities that you are looking for. We will start off introducing a product by giving a gist of the technical capability that we need to address, then introduce you briefly to the product.

In this chapter we will cover the following topics:

- Remember-me authentication
- Session management
- CSRF
- CSP
- Channel security
- CORS Support
- The Crypto module
- Secret management
- HTTP Data Integrity Validator
- Custom DSL

Remember-me authentication

We will be reusing and enhancing the example that we built in Chapter 2, *Deep Diving into Spring Security* (jetty-db-basic-authentication), to explain how Spring Security can be used to achieve remember me, or persistent login, functionality. In the example that we are going to reuse, we have used basic authentication, in which user credentials are stored in a MySQL database.

Remember me functionality is achieved in Spring Security by sending cookies to the browser when the user chooses to remember his/her credentials on the client side. The cookie can be configured to be stored in the browser for a stipulated time. If the cookie exists and is valid, the next time the user accesses the application, they are taken straight to the user's home page and avoid explicit authentication with a username/password combination.

Remember me functionality can be achieved using two approaches:

- **Hash-based tokens**: Username, expiry time, password, and a private key are hashed and send to the client as a token
- **Persistent tokens**: A persistent storage mechanism is used to store the token on the server

We will now go through a simple implementation of the persistent token approach to explain this concept in detail.

Creating a new table in MySQL database

We will use the same schema as the MySQL DB that we used in Chapter 2, *Deep Diving into Spring Security*. Keep everything as is, and then create a new table in the MySQL database for storing persistent tokens by executing the following DDL statement in the MySQL workbench:

```
create table persistent_logins(
    series varchar(64) not null primary key,
    username varchar(75) not null,
    token varchar(100) not null,
    last_used timestamp not null
);
```

Spring Security configuration

In `Chapter 2`, *Deep Diving into Spring Security* (in the Spring Security setup sub-section of the `Sample` application section), we saw basic authentication, which we configured in our configure method in the Spring Security Configuration class. In this example, we will create a custom login page and change the login mechanism to form-based. Open the `SpringSecurityConfig` class and change the configure method, as shown in the following code snippet. Then, add the `tokenRepository` bean that we are going to use to accomplish remember me functionality:

```
@Override
protected void configure(HttpSecurity http) throws Exception {
  http.csrf().disable();
  http.authorizeRequests().anyRequest().hasAnyRole("ADMIN", "USER")
      .and()
      .authorizeRequests().antMatchers("/login**").permitAll()
      .and()
      .formLogin()
      .loginPage("/login").loginProcessingUrl("/loginProc").permitAll()
      .and()
      .logout().logoutSuccessUrl("/login").permitAll()
      .and()
      .rememberMe()
.rememberMeParameter("rememberme").tokenRepository(tokenRepository());
}
@Bean
public PersistentTokenRepository tokenRepository() {
  JdbcTokenRepositoryImpl jdbcTokenRepositoryImpl=new
JdbcTokenRepositoryImpl();
  jdbcTokenRepositoryImpl.setDataSource(dataSource);
  return jdbcTokenRepositoryImpl;
}
```

The custom login page

Create a new page, namely `login.jsp` in the `src/main/webapp/WEB-INF/view` folder. The main section of the page, containing the `username`, `password`, and `rememberme` fields, is as shown in the following code snippet:

```
<form action='<spring:url value="/loginProc"/>' method="post">
  <table>
    <tr>
        <td>Username</td>
        <td><input type="text" name="username"></td>
    </tr>
```

```
        <tr>
            <td>Password</td>
            <td><input type="password" name="password"></td>
        </tr>
        <tr>
            <td><input type="checkbox" name="rememberme"></td>
            <td>Remember me</td>
        </tr>
        <tr>
            <td><button type="submit">Login</button></td>
        </tr>
    </table>
</form>
```

Make sure that you name the remember me checkbox the same as you specified in the Spring Security configuration.

Running the application and testing

Run the project by executing the following command:

```
mvn jetty:run
```

Wait for the console to print **[INFO] Started Jetty Server**.

Open a browser (I use Firefox in private mode for testing) and navigate to `http://localhost:8080`, and you will be shown the custom login page that you created, as shown in the following screenshot:

Figure 1: The custom login page

Enter `user/user@password` as the username and password. Click on `Remember me` and click the `Login` button, and you will be navigated to the user home page, as shown here:

Figure 2: User home page

Query your MySQL database for the `persistent_logins` table, and you will see a new record, as shown in the following screenshot:

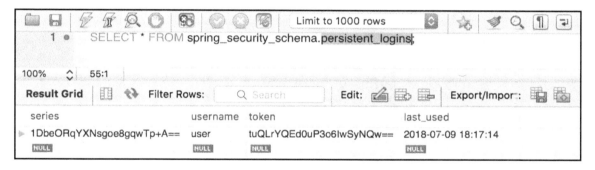

Figure 3: MySQLWorkbench querying new persistent_logins table

Now, go to the developer tools in your browser and check for cookies. Depending on the browser that you are using, you should see something similar to this:

Figure 4: Browser cookie set to achieve remember-me functionality

The entire project for this example can be found at the book's GitHub page in the `jetty-db-basic-authentication-remember-me` project.

Session management

Spring Security allows you to manage sessions on your server with only some configuration. Some of the most important session management activities are listed here:

- **Session creation**: This decides when a session needs to be created and the ways in which you can interact with it. In the Spring Security configuration, put in the following code:

  ```
  http.sessionManagement().sessionCreationPolicy(SessionCreationPolicy.ALWAYS);
  ```

  There are four session creation policies that you can choose from. They are as follows:

    - `ALWAYS`: Always create a session if it doesn't exist.
    - `IF_REQUIRED`: If required, a session is created.
    - `NEVER`: This will never create a session; rather, it will use the session if it exists.
    - `STATELESS`: No session will be created nor used.
    - `invalidSession`: This controls how the user is intimated if the server sees an invalid session:

    ```
    http.sessionManagement().invalidSessionUrl("/invalidSession");
    ```

- **Session timeout**: This controls how the user is intimated if the session has expired.
- **Concurrent session**: This allows control over how many sessions a user can start in an application. If the maximum sessions is set as 1, when the user logs in for the second time, the previous session is invalidated and the user is logged out. If the value specified is greater than 1, the user is allowed to have that many sessions concurrently:

  ```
  http.sessionManagement().maximumSessions(1);
  ```

The following screenshot shows the default error screen, that pops up when more than the desired amount of sessions (as configured) are created by the same user:

Figure 5: Error thrown when a user accesses multiple sessions

- **Session fixation**: This is very similar to concurrent session control. This setting allows us to control what will happen when a new session is initiated by a user. We can specify the following three values:
    - `migrateSession`: On the creation of a new session after successful authentication, the old session is invalidated and all attributes are copied to the new session:

    ```
    http.sessionManagement().sessionFixation().migrateSession()
    ;
    ```

    - `newSession`: A new session is created without copying any of the attributes from the previous valid session:

    ```
    http.sessionManagement().sessionFixation().newSession();
    ```

    - `none`: The old session is reused and is not invalidated:

    ```
    http.sessionManagement().sessionFixation().none()
    ```

CSRF

Cross-Site Request Forgery (**CSRF**) (`https://www.owasp.org/index.php/Cross-Site_Request_Forgery_(CSRF)`) is an attack that forces an end user to execute unwanted actions on a web application in which they're currently authenticated. CSRF attacks specifically target state-changing requests, not theft of data, since the attacker has no way to see the response to the forged request.

The **Open Web Application Security Project** (**OWASP**) considers CSRF as one of the most common security risks for web applications. OWASP publishes a list (known as the OWASP Top 10) every year, highlighting the top 10 security risks plaguing web applications—it considers CSRF to be in fifth position.

In Spring Security, CSRF is enabled by default. If needs be (we have disabled this in many of our examples so that we are able to concentrate on the main concept that the examples are supposed to convey), we can disable it explicitly by adding the following code snippet in your Spring Security configuration:

```
http
    .csrf().disable();
```

Even though CSRF is enabled by default, for it to function, each request needs to provide a CSRF token. If a CSRF token is not sent across to the server, the server will reject the request and throw an error. If you are using **Java Server Page** (**JSP**) as your view, just by including hidden input, as shown in the following code snippet, many things would happen auto-magically:

```
<input type="hidden" name="${_csrf.parameterName}" value="${_csrf.token}" />
```

If you are using an AJAX request to call a server, instead of hidden input, you can supply the CSRF token in the form of an HTTP header. You can declare the CSRF-related header as meta tags, as shown in the following code snippet:

```
<head>
    <meta name="_csrf" content="${_csrf.token}"/>
    <meta name="_csrf_header" content="${_csrf.headerName}"/>
    <!-- ... -->
</head>
```

After that, while calling the server, include these (_csrf and _csrf_header) as headers and you will be allowed to call the required endpoints.

If you would like to persist the CSRF token, Spring Security allows you to do this by tweaking the configuration as shown in the following code snippet:

```
http
    .csrf()
    .csrfTokenRepository(new CookieCsrfTokenRepository());
```

While doing this, the CSRF token is persisted as a cookie, which can be read by the server and validated (all done auto-magically).

CSP

Content Security Policy (**CSP**) (https://developer.mozilla.org/en-US/docs/Web/HTTP/CSP) is an added layer of security that helps to detect and mitigate certain types of attacks, including **Cross Site Scripting** (**XSS**) and data injection attacks. These attacks are used for everything from data theft to site defacement or distribution of malware.

A proper CSP setup in your application can handle content injection vulnerabilities, and is a great way to reduce XSS. XSS stands at number two in the OWASP Top 10.

A CSP is not a solution to handling all injection vulnerabilities, but can be used as one of the tools to reduce injection attacks to a reasonable level.

CSP is a declarative policy, implemented using HTTP headers. It can be run in an application in two modes:

- Production mode (declared as CSP)
- Report-only mode (used for testing and are declared as *Content-Security-Policy-Report-Only*)

CSP contains a set of security policy directives responsible for putting appropriate restrictions on a web resource and then informing the client (user agent) accordingly when breached. For example, the following security policy snippet loads scripts from the defined trusted domains:

```
Content-Security-Policy: script-src https://trusted-domain.com
```

If there's a breach, the user agent will block it, and if the policy specifies a `report-uri` parameter, as shown in the following example, it will report the violation in the form of JSON to that URI:

```
Content-Security-Policy: script-src https://trusted-domain.com; report-uri
/csp-report-api/
```

The previous examples showcase CSP working in production mode. If you would like to first test the security policy and after a particular period of time make those policies in production mode, CSP provides a mechanism for that, as shown in the following code snippet:

```
Content-Security-Policy-Report-Only: script-src https://trusted-domain.com;
report-uri /csp-report-api/
```

In report-only mode, when a breach is detected, the report is posted to the `report-uri` in JSON format, as shown in the following code:

```
{"csp-report":
    {"document-uri":"...",
    "violated-directive":"script-src https://trusted-domain.com",
    "original-policy":"...",
    "blocked-uri":"https://untrusted-domain.com"}
}
```

Apart from the security directives detailed in the preceding examples, there are a number of security directives that can be used while setting up your CSP. For a full list of directives, please refer to `https://content-security-policy.com/`.

In a similar way to CSRF tokens, CSP can also be used to make sure that specific resources contain a token while accessing the server. The following example shows the use of this nonce approach:

```
Content-Security-Policy: script-src 'self' 'nonce-<cryptographically
generated random string>'
```

Similar to a CSRF token, this nonce has to be included along with any resource access in the server, and this has to be newly generated while a page is loaded.

CSP also allows you to load the resources only if they match the hash that the server expects. The following policy is used to achieve this:

```
Content-Security-Policy: script-src 'self' 'sha256-<base64 encoded hash>'
```

CSP is supported by almost all modern browsers. Even if some security directives are not supported by certain browsers, other supported directives will work without any problem. The best way to handle that is to send only the security directives that will definitely be supported by the browser by deciphering the user agent, rather than throwing errors on the client.

CSP using Spring Security

Configuring CSP using Spring Security configuration is a breeze. By default, CSP is not enabled. You can enable it in Spring Security configuration, as shown in the following code snippet:

```
http
     .headers()
          .contentSecurityPolicy("script-src 'self'
https://trusted-domain.com; report-uri /csp-report-api/");
```

The report-only CSP in the Spring Security configuration is as follows:

```
http
     .headers()
          .contentSecurityPolicy("script-src 'self'
https://trusted-domain.com; report-uri /csp-report-api/")
          .reportOnly();
```

Channel security

In addition to authentication and authorization, Spring Security can also be used to check for any additional property presence for each request reaching the server. It can check for protocol (transport type, HTTP, or HTTPS), presence of certain HTTP headers, and more. SSL is now the de facto standard for any web application (or website) to comply with, and many search engines (such as Google, for example) even penalize you if your website is not HTTPS. SSL is made use of in securing the channel on which data flows from client to server and vice versa.

Spring Security can be configured to explicitly check for URL patterns and explicitly redirect the user to HTTPS if they are coming with the HTTP protocol.

This can be easily done by configuring the appropriate URL pattern in your Spring Security configuration, as shown here:

```
http.authorizeRequests()
     .requiresChannel().antMatchers("/httpsRequired/**").requiresSecure();
```

When users access the /httpsRequired/** URL pattern and if the protocol is HTTP, Spring Security will redirect the user to the same URL with the HTTPS protocol. The following configuration is used to secure all requests:

```
http.authorizeRequests()
     .requiresChannel().anyRequest().requiresSecure();
```

To explicitly mention certain URLs as insecure, use the following code:

```
.requiresChannel().antMatchers("/httpRequired/**").requiresInsecure();
```

The following code snippet shows how to specify any request to be HTTP (insecure):

```
.requiresChannel().anyRequest().requiresInsecure();
```

CORS Support

Cross-Origin Resource Sharing (CORS) (`https://developer.mozilla.org/en-US/docs/Web/HTTP/CORS`) is a mechanism that uses additional HTTP headers to tell a browser to let a web application running at one origin (domain) have permission to access selected resources from a server at a different origin. A web application makes a cross-origin HTTP request when it requests a resource that has a different origin (domain, protocol, and port) than its own origin.

We won't be creating full-fledged projects in this section to explain the working of CORS. We will use code snippets and will explain each bit of code so that the section is concise.

Change your Spring Security configuration, as shown in the following code snippet:

```
@EnableWebSecurity
@Configuration
public class SpringSecurityConfig extends WebSecurityConfigurerAdapter {

  @Override
  protected void configure(HttpSecurity http) throws Exception {
    http.cors();
  }
  @Bean
  CorsConfigurationSource corsConfigurationSource() {
    UrlBasedCorsConfigurationSource urlCorsConfigSrc = new
        UrlBasedCorsConfigurationSource();
    urlCorsConfigSrc.registerCorsConfiguration("/**",
      new CorsConfiguration().applyPermitDefaultValues());
    return urlCorsConfigSrc;
  }
}
```

In the preceding code, we configure CORS in the Spring Security `configure` method. We then create a new bean, `corsConfigurationSource`, in which we enable the `/**` path to be accessible by other domains. This is not really ideal in many scenarios, and the following code snippet shows the more enhanced `CorsConfiguration` class:

```
CorsConfiguration configuration = new CorsConfiguration();
configuration.setAllowedOrigins(new ArrayList<String>(Arrays.asList("*")));
configuration.setAllowedHeaders(new ArrayList<String>
    (Arrays.asList("Authorization", "Cache-Control", "Content-Type")));
configuration.setAllowedMethods(new ArrayList<String>(Arrays.asList("HEAD",
    "GET", "POST", "PUT", "DELETE", "PATCH")));
configuration.setAllowCredentials(true);
```

If it is a Spring MVC application, you can have a Spring MVC configuration file in which you can specify CORS mapping by creating a bean, as shown here:

```
@Configuration
public class SpringMVCConfig {
  @Bean
  public WebMvcConfigurer corsConfigurer() {
    return new WebMvcConfigurer() {
      @Override
      public void addCorsMappings(CorsRegistry registry) {
        registry.addMapping("/**")
          .allowedMethods("HEAD", "GET", "PUT", "POST", "DELETE",
            "PATCH","OPTIONS");
      }
    };
  }
}
```

I have copied a previous example from Chapter 2, *Deep Diving into Spring Security*, and created a new project in this chapter, containing full source code in `spring-boot-in-memory-basic-authentication-with-cors`. What we have done here is set the CORS global configuration by declaring the `CorsConfigurationSource` bean.

The Crypto module

The Spring Security Crypto module allows you to do password encoding, symmetric encryption, and key generation. The module is bundled as part of the core Spring Security offering with no dependency upon other Spring Security code.

Password encoding

Modernized password encoding is one of the new features of Spring Security 5. Spring Security's `PasswordEncoder` interface is central to it and does one-way hashing of passwords using various algorithms, which can then be stored securely. Spring Security supports a number of password-encoding algorithms:

- `BcryptPasswordEncoder`: This uses the Bcrypt strong hash function. You can optionally supply the strength parameter (default value is 10); the higher the value, the more work has to be done to hash the password.
- `Pbkdf2PasswordEncoder`: This uses **Password-Based Key Derivation Function 2 (PKDF2)** with a configurable number of iterations and an 8-byte random salt value.
- `ScryptPasswordEncoder`: This uses the Scrypt hashing function. While hashing, clients can supply a CPU cost parameter, a memory cost parameter, and a parallelization parameter. The current implementation uses the Bouncy Castle library.

Encryption

Spring Security's `org.springframework.security.crypto.encrypt.Encryptors` class has factory methods that can be used to create symmetric encryptors. The class supports two encryptors:

- `BytesEncryptor`: The service interface for symmetric data encryption of data in the form of raw byte arrays.
- `TextEncryptor`: The service interface for symmetric data encryption of text strings:

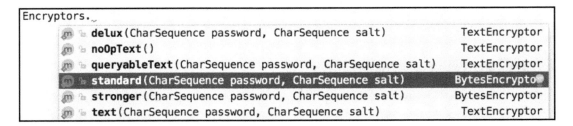

```
Encryptors.
    m   delux(CharSequence password, CharSequence salt)                        TextEncryptor
    m   noOpText()                                                             TextEncryptor
    m   queryableText(CharSequence password, CharSequence salt)                TextEncryptor
    m   standard(CharSequence password, CharSequence salt)                     BytesEncrypto
    m   stronger(CharSequence password, CharSequence salt)                     BytesEncryptor
    m   text(CharSequence password, CharSequence salt)                         TextEncryptor
```

Key generation

As seen in the previous section on encryption, Spring Security has a class, namely `org.springframework.security.crypto.keygen.KeyGenerators`, that has a number of factory methods that can used to construct a number of keys needed for your application.

The following are the two supported types of key generator:

- `BytesKeyGenerator`: The generator for generating unique byte array-based keys.
- `StringKeyGenerator`: The generator for unique string keys:

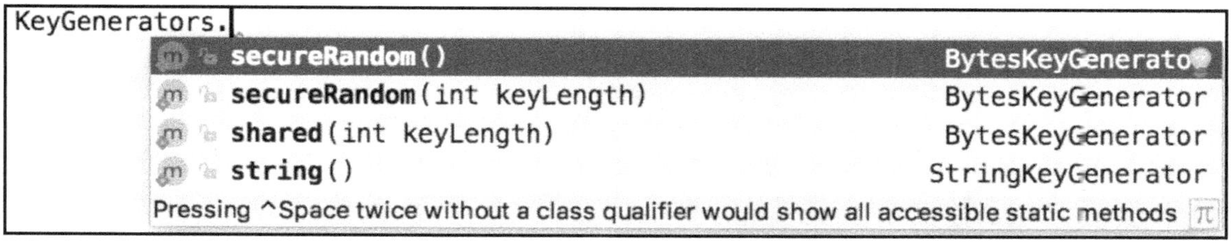

Figure 7: The BytesKeyGenerator and StringKeyGenerator factory methods

Secret management

In an application, we need to handle a variety of secret/secure data in the form of API keys, other application passwords, and more. Often, for an application deployed and running in a production environment, keeping these in plain text can result in security breaches. With automation up for grabs quite cheaply nowadays, for modern applications, storing such data securely with access control and secure storage is a must.

Encryption is something that has been widely embraced, but for decryption, a key needs to be circulated, and this circulation of the key is usually a big problem. If a person decides to take the key outside of the organization, there can be serious problems.

Vault from HashiCorp is a very strong contender as a solution to this issue, and helps in managing these secrets easily with very rigid controls. It provides APIs that give access based on set policies. It also has the capability to provide access control, and it also comes with encryption functionality out of box. In addition, it has a variety of persistent backend supports, such as Consul (from HashiCorp), and more, making it easy for enterprises to adopt it. Vault is written in Go and has binaries available for many platforms, and can be downloaded from its website. In this section, we will quickly run you through the Vault product itself, and then go through an example in which we will create a Spring Boot project and securely access some of the secrets stored in the Vault. Without further ado, let's get our hands dirty with actual code.

Starting by unsealing Vault

Download the latest binary from the Vault project's website (https://www.vaultproject. io/downloads.html), according to your operating system, and install it. To start Vault, you need to have a file—vault.conf—in which we will specify some of the options that are needed for Vault to start. Here is a sample vault.conf file that you can use:

```
backend "inmem" {
}
listener "tcp" {
  address = "0.0.0.0:8200"
  tls_disable = 1
}
disable_mlock = true
```

In the vault.conf file, we explicitly set the address that it will listen to and also disable TLS/SSL (so that it runs in plain text mode).

Start Vault by specifying the location of the vault.conf file with the following command:

```
./vault server -config vault.conf
```

As you can see from the screenshot below, Vault is running in plain text mode (with TLS/SSL disabled):

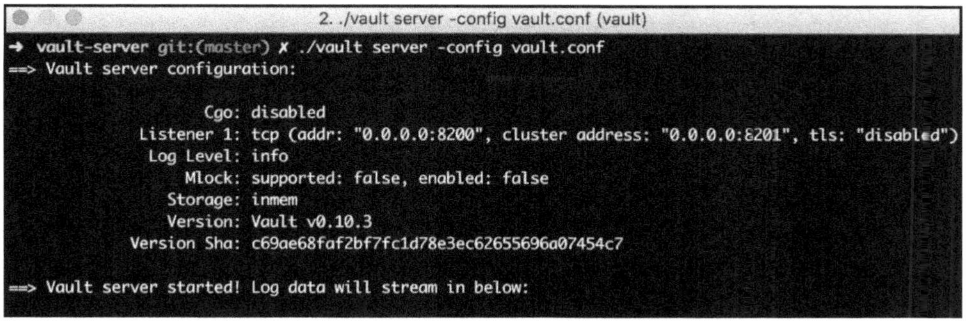

Figure 8: Starting and configuring Vault

Open a new command prompt, which is where we will now start administering Vault. Set an environment variable by executing the following command to let the clients know that they have to use plain text to connect to Vault (as we have disabled TLS/SSL):

```
export VAULT_ADDR=http://127.0.0.1:8200
```

After this, initialize Vault key generation by executing the following command:

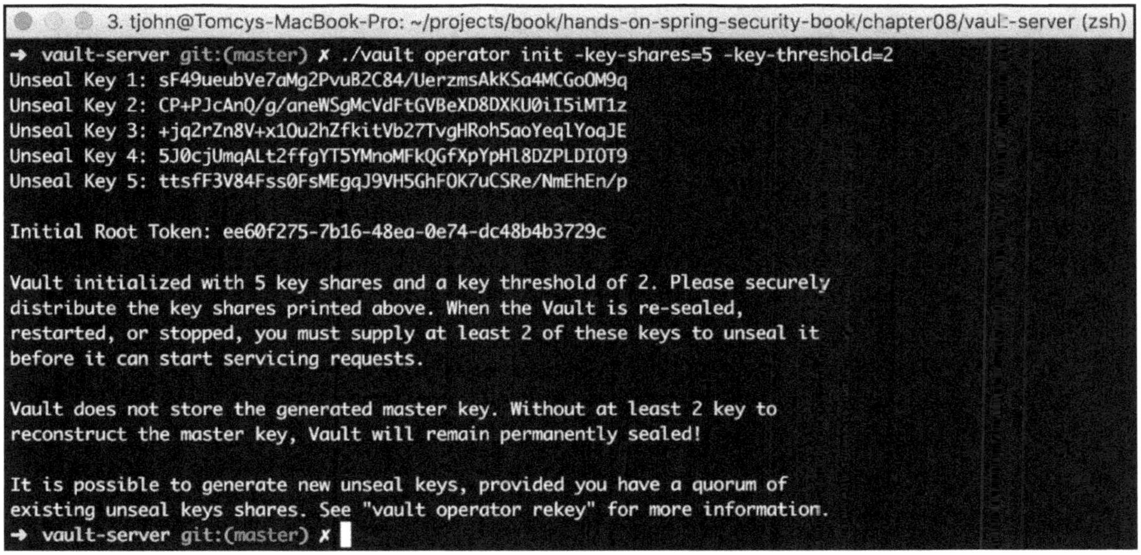

Figure 9: Initializing Vault

The command that we have used gave us five key shares and a key threshold of two. It's important to note that we cannot change these values once Vault is initialized (output is shown only once). Be careful to gather the necessary information; otherwise, you will not be able to retrieve any data stored in Vault. As you can see from the preceding screenshot, the `init` command of Vault gives us the keys and token that are needed to unseal Vault. Before we can use Vault, it has to be unsealed.

Unsealing (`https://www.vaultproject.io/docs/concepts/seal.html`) is the process of constructing the master key necessary to read the decryption key to decrypt the data, allowing access to the Vault. Prior to unsealing, almost no operations are possible with Vault.

You can unseal Vault by executing the following command and providing any of the keys generated during the Vault initialization process:

```
./vault unseal <any key generated using initialization>
```

The following screenshot shows the successful execution of the preceding command:

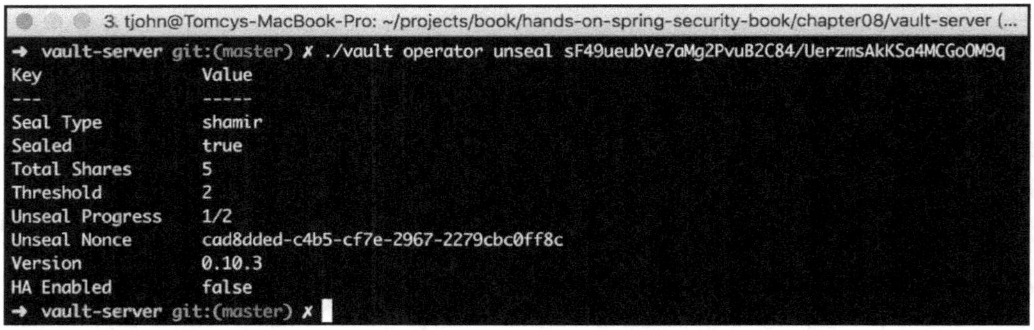

Figure 10: Unsealing Vault

Once it is unsealed, your Vault is now ready to store the secret data that you may want to use in your application.

After you have successfully unsealed Vault, to store any data, you first need to authenticate. When we initialized Vault, we were shown a token (on the screen), and this token is used to authenticate. One of the easiest ways to achieve authentication using this token is to set up a new environment variable (`VAULT_TOKEN`). Execute the following command as shown, and when Vault starts, it will make use of this environment variable and authenticate itself:

```
export VAULT_TOKEN=ee60f275-7b16-48ea-0e74-dc48b4b3729c
```

Once the preceding command is executed, you can now write your secret by executing the following command:

```
./vault write secret/movie-application password=randomstring
```

After you enter the command, you should receive the following output:

Figure 11: Writing a secret to your Vault

Tokens are the primary way in which authentication is done in Vault. Besides that, there are other mechanisms, such as LDAP and username/password, with which authentication can be done.

The Spring Boot project

Spring has a dedicated module, called Spring Cloud Vault, that makes use of Vault in your application a breeze. Spring Cloud Vault is very easy to use, and we will be covering how to use it in this section.

Spring Cloud Vault Config (`http://cloud.spring.io/spring-cloud-vault/`) provides client-side support for externalized configuration in a distributed system. With HashiCorp's Vault you have a central place to manage external secret properties for applications across all environments. Vault can manage static and dynamic secrets such as username/password for remote applications/resources and provide credentials for external services such as MySQL, PostgreSQL, Apache Cassandra, MongoDB, Consul, AWS, and more.

We will be using the Spring Boot project (generated using Spring Initializr, `https://start.spring.io`). At the start of the application, Vault is started and all the secrets are picked up:

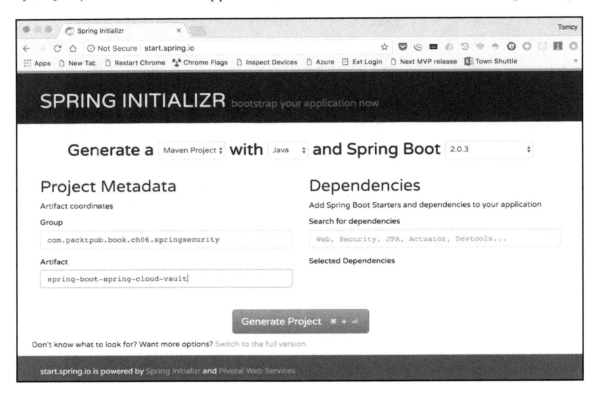

Figure 12: Creation of an empty Spring Initializr project

Unzip the downloaded Spring Initializr project by executing the following command:

```
unzip -a spring-boot-spring-cloud-vault.zip
```

Import the project in your favorite IDE (I am using IntelliJ).

The Maven dependency

Make sure that your project's pom.xml has the following Maven dependency added:

```
<dependency>
 <groupId>org.springframework.cloud</groupId>
 <artifactId>spring-cloud-starter-vault-config</artifactId>
 <version>2.0.0.RELEASE</version>
</dependency>
```

When the Spring Boot project starts, it will pick the default Vault configuration if the Vault server is running on port 8200. If you want to customize these properties, you can specify bootstrap.yml or bootstrap.properties. In our example, we will explicitly set the bootstrap.yml file with the following content:

```
spring:
  application:
      name: movie-application
spring.cloud.vault:
  host: localhost # hostname of vault server
  port: 8200  # vault server port
  scheme: http # connection scheme http or https
  uri: http://localhost:8200 # vault endpoint
  connection-timeout: 10000 # connection timeout in milliseconds
  read-timeout: 5000  # read timeout in milliseconds
  config:
      order: -10  # order for property source
  token: ee60f275-7b16-48ea-0e74-dc48b4b3729c
health.vault.enabled: true  # health endpoint enabled using spring actuator
```

We will be using the HTTP scheme, as we started Vault in plain text mode. If you would like to use HTTPS, it's quite easy to do so, as most things are done through scripts already provided. This is the default scheme in which Vault runs, and this is how it has to be in the production setup. Let's understand this concept first before going into a bit more depth when you implement the actual use case.

If you would like to run Vault in the HTTPS scheme, Spring Cloud Vault has a number of scripts available in its source code under `src/test/bash` (`https://github.com/spring-cloud/spring-cloud-vault/tree/master/src/test/bash`) that can be used to create the necessary certificates and then run Vault in this scheme. To keep this section concise, we won't be covering this aspect in much more detail here.

In the `.yml` file, we have used the root token that was created as part of the initialization of Vault. If you need to, you can get a new token by executing the following command:

```
./vault token create
```

The following screenshot shows the successful execution of the `token create` command:

Figure 13: New Vault token creation

In your Spring Boot project, add the following code snippet in your application run class, `SpringBootSpringCloudVaultApplication`:

```
@Value("${password}")
String password;

@PostConstruct
private void postConstruct() {
  System.out.println("Secret in Movie application password is: " +
password);
}
```

In this code, the `password` field will be filled by Spring Cloud Vault, and if you run the application (using command `mvn spring-boot:run`), you should see that Spring Cloud Vault connects to the running Vault (using the configuration in the `bootstrap.yml` file) and retrieves the value that we wrote to Vault for `movie-application`.

This concludes our look at a base application using Spring Boot and Spring Cloud Vault. You can see the full source in the book's GitHub page in the project under this chapter, named `spring-boot-spring-cloud-vault`.

HTTP Data Integrity Validator

Spring Security aids us in enriching our application with common security features, allowing us to do so very easily and with minimal code. However, Spring Security is slowly and steadily catching up with many of the additional security features needed in modern applications. Most of these applications are deployed on the cloud and have very high rates of changes pushed to production on a day-to-day basis. **HTTP Data Integrity Validator** (**HDIV**) is a product that can be used to further enrich your application security.

What is HDIV?

HDIV was originally born as an open source project when it was developed by Roberto Velasco, Gotzon Illarramendi, and Gorka Vicente to confront security issues detected in production environments. The first stable Version 1.0 was released in 2008, in the form of a security library to be integrated within web applications. HDIV was officially integrated with Spring MVC, the most-used Java solution for web application development in 2011. In 2012, HDIV was integrated with Grails. In 2015, HDIV was included within Spring Framework official documentation as a solution related to web security. Based on global interest and responding to high market demand, the creators founded the **HDIV Security** (https://hdivsecurity.com/) company and launched the commercial version of HDIV in 2016. HDIV solutions are built into applications during development to deliver the strongest available **Runtime Application Self Protection** (**RASP**) against the OWASP Top 10 threats.

HDIV was born to protect applications against parameter-tampering attacks. Its first purpose (looking at the acronym) was to guarantee the integrity (no data modification) of all the data generated by the server (links, hidden fields, combo values, radio buttons, destiny pages, cookies, headers, and more). HDIV extends a web application's behavior by adding security functionalities, as well as maintaining the API and the framework specification. HDIV gradually incorporated capabilities such as CSRF, **SQL Injection** (**SQLi**), and XSS protection, thus offering greatly increased security and being more than just an HTTP data integrity validator.

Attacks are becoming lower in cost and more automated. Manual security testing is becoming a costly bottleneck. Spring Security protects the application by easily implementing the most important security aspects, such as authentication and authorization, but does not protect from common security bugs and design flaws in your application code. This is where integrating a Spring application that is already secured using Spring Security can bring in HDIV. We will be going through a very simple example, which will showcase a few of the areas where HDIV shines. Here are some of those advantages, as detailed by their website:

- HDIV detects security bugs in source code before it is exploited, using a runtime dataflow technique to report the file and line number of the vulnerability. Reporting is immediate to developers during the development process either within the web browser or within a centralized web console.

- It protects from business logic flaws with no need to learn applications and offers detection and protection from security bugs without changing the source code.
- HDIV makes integration possible between the pen-testing tool (Burp Suite) and the application, communicating valuable information to the pen-tester. It avoids many hand-coded steps, focusing the attention and effort of pen-testers on the most vulnerable entry points.

 For more information, you can check the following link: `https://hdivsecurity.com/`.

Let's start building a simple example that showcases the protection that HDIV does by protecting links and form data in your application.

The Bootstrap project

We will be using a base project created out of Spring Initializr for creating our HDIV sample, as shown here:

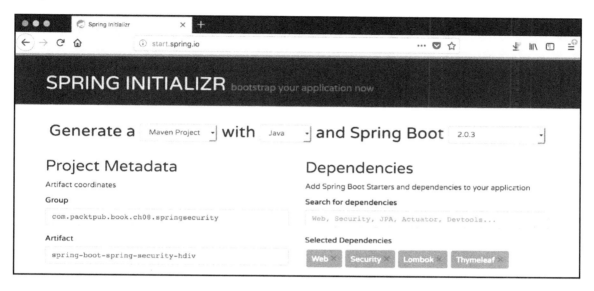

Figure 14: Basic Spring Initializr project setup

Maven dependencies

In the following code, we are calling out explicit dependency that we need as part of this project, which is HDIV:

```
<!--HDIV dependency-->
<dependency>
    <groupId>org.hdiv</groupId>
    <artifactId>spring-boot-starter-hdiv-thymeleaf</artifactId>
    <version>1.3.1</version>
    <type>pom</type>
</dependency>
```

HDIV has support for a number of web application frameworks. In our example, we'll be using Spring MVC along with Thymeleaf and above mentioned dependency takes care of this.

Spring Security configuration

By now, you will already know what goes in the Spring Security configuration file. We will have in-memory authentication and will be configuring two users (similar to what we have been doing all throughout this book). We will have form-based login and also will be creating our own login page.

Spring MVC configuration

The Spring MVC configuration that we have been looking at so far is very basic. There isn't anything worth a special mention here. We will just need to ensure that the controller attached to the login page is explicitly defined.

HDIV configuration

This magic class will bring in HDIV capability to your application without too much trouble. The full class is as shown here:

```
@Configuration
@EnableHdivWebSecurity
public class HdivSecurityConfig extends HdivWebSecurityConfigurerAdapter {
    @Override
    public void addExclusions(final ExclusionRegistry registry) {
        registry.addUrlExclusions("/login");
    }
}
```

The heavy lifting is done by the class that we are extending, `HdivWebSecurityConfigurerAdapter`. Also, the `@EnableHdivWebSecurity` annotation makes sure that much of the setup is automatically taken care of. We just need to make sure that the configuration of our login page URL is excluded from HDIV security by overriding the `addExclusions` method.

The Model class

We will be using the same model class we have been using throughout this book—`Movie`. To ease coding, we will be using the Lombok library, which does all the magic by looking at the various annotations configured in the class.

The Controller class

We will just have one controller class, where we will map all the pages that we are going to create in this example. To showcase the power of HDIV, we will see HDIV in action for two cases:

- A movie creation page (movie bean), showing HDIV at work in a page containing a form
- A links page that shows HDIV intercepting and throwing errors when someone manipulates the actual link

The class is quite straightforward and doesn't need to be detailed here.

Pages

As mentioned before, we will have the following pages created in our example:

- login.html: The custom login page that we will use for users to log in to the application
- main.html: The page that the user navigates to after successful login, containing links to the movie creation and links pages
- links.html: The page that the user is navigated to when they click on the links URL
- movie.html: The movie creation page, containing two fields—title and genre

Running the application

Run the application just like any other Spring Boot project by executing the following command:

```
mvn spring-boot:run
```

Go to a browser and navigate to `http://localhost:8080` and you will be presented with a login page, as shown here:

Figure 15: Login page

As shown in the preceding screenshot, enter the `username/password` and click on the **Login** button, and you will be navigated to the home page:

Figure 16: The home page, which is presented to the user after successful login

Click on the link to navigate to the page where you can create a new movie. You will be navigated to the page shown in the following screenshot. Look closely at the URL and you will see a new query parameter has been added, _HDIV_STATE_. The server validates and ensures that the submitted form is genuine by looking at that value

Figure 17: The Create Movie screen, showing off the _HDIV_STATE_ query string

Now go back to the home page and click on the links page. You will be navigated to the following page:

Figure 18: The links page, showing the _HDIV_STATE_ query string

As stated in the page, try manipulating the link (change the `_HDIV_STATE_` value) and you will be taken to the HDIV error page:

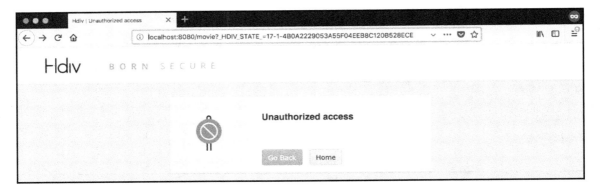

Figure 19: The HDIV error page, which displays in the case of error conditions

This example showcases just two of the cases where HDIV shows its worth when working alongside Spring Security. For more details, I urge you to look at the HDIV website and documentation, which is available here:

- `https://hdivsecurity.com/docs/`
- `https://hdivsecurity.com/docs/installation/library-setup/`
- `https://github.com/hdiv/hdiv`

Custom DSL

Spring Security allows you to write your own **Domain Specific Language** (**DSL**), which can be used to configure security in your application. We have already seen a custom DSL in action when we implemented SAML authentication using OKTA. We used an OKTA-provided custom DSL to configure Spring Security.

To write your own custom DSL, you can extend the `AbstractHttpConfigurer` *class* and override a few of it's methods, as shown here:

```
public class CustomDSL extends AbstractHttpConfigurer<CustomDSL,
HttpSecurity> {
    @Override
    public void init(HttpSecurity builder) throws Exception {
        // Any configurations that you would like to do (say as default) can
be
        configured here
```

```
    }

    @Override
    public void configure(HttpSecurity builder) throws Exception {
        // Can add anything specific to your application and this will be
honored
    }
}
```

In your Spring Security configuration class (the configure method), you can then use your custom DSL, as shown here:

```
@Override
  protected void configure(HttpSecurity http) throws Exception {
      http
          .apply(<invoke custom DSL>)
          ...;
}
```

When Spring Security sees a custom DSL setup, the execution of code is as follows:

1. Invoke the Spring Security configuration class's `configure` method
2. Invoke the custom DSL `init` method
3. Invoke the custom DSL `configure` method

Spring Security uses this approach to implement `authorizeRequests()`.

Summary

This chapter introduced you to some of the other capabilities of Spring Security that can be used in your application. Using examples, we covered how to achieve remember-me functionality in your application. We also touched briefly upon concepts such as CSRF, CORS, CSP, channel security, and session management. We also covered the Crypto module in Spring Security concisely.

We wrapped up the chapter by introducing two products that can work along with Spring Security—HashiCorp Vault (for secret management) and HDIV (for additional security features).

After reading this chapter, you should have a clear understanding of some of the additional features that can be implemented using Spring Security. You should also have a good understanding of some of the products that can be used alongside Spring Security to achieve some of the most important technical capabilities that are needed for modern applications.

Now, pat yourself your back if you are reading this, as with this chapter, we complete the book. I hope you have enjoyed every bit of this book, and I hope you have learned something new that can be used for creating wonderful and innovative new applications.

Thank you for reading!

Other Books You May Enjoy

If you enjoyed this book, you may be interested in these other books by Packt:

Spring Boot 2.0 Cookbook - Second Edition
Alex Antonov

ISBN: 978-1-78712-982-5

- Get to know Spring Boot Starters and create custom auto-configurations
- Work with custom annotations that enable bean activation
- Use DevTools to easily develop and debug applications
- Learn the effective testing techniques by integrating Cucumber and Spock
- Observe an eternal application configuration using Consul
- Move your existing Spring Boot applications to the cloud
- Use Hashicorp Consul and Netflix Eureka for dynamic Service Discovery
- Understand the various mechanisms that Spring Boot provides to examine an application's health

Mastering Spring Boot 2.0
Dinesh Rajput

ISBN: 978-1-78712-756-2

- Build logically structured and highly maintainable Spring Boot applications
- Configure RESTful microservices using Spring Boot
- Make the application production and operation-friendly with Spring Actuator
- Build modern, high-performance distributed applications using cloud patterns
- Manage and deploy your Spring Boot application to the cloud (AWS)
- Monitor distributed applications using log aggregation and ELK

Leave a review - let other readers know what you think

Please share your thoughts on this book with others by leaving a review on the site that you bought it from. If you purchased the book from Amazon, please leave us an honest review on this book's Amazon page. This is vital so that other potential readers can see and use your unbiased opinion to make purchasing decisions, we can understand what our customers think about our products, and our authors can see your feedback on the title that they have worked with Packt to create. It will only take a few minutes of your time, but is valuable to other potential customers, our authors, and Packt. Thank you!

Index

www.ingramcontent.com/pod-product-compliance
Lightning Source LLC
LaVergne TN
LVHW081520050326
832903LV00025B/1559